Conquer *New S...*

Informational Text

MW01140304

Table of Contents

Introduction

Many states have adopted standards that set clear expectations about what students need to learn at each grade level. The standards are designed to be rigorous and pertinent to the real world, and they reflect the knowledge and skills that our young people need for success in college and careers.

Why *Conquer New Standards: Informational Text?*
As a teacher, you are required to incorporate these standards into your lesson plans. Your students may need targeted practice in order to meet grade-level standards and be promoted to the next grade.

Conquer New Standards: Informational Text provides you with ready-to-go units that support students in the development of key skills outlined in the standards (see the chart on page 5). Each unit includes one or more passages as well as a model of a response to a question about that passage. After reading the passage and reviewing the model, students practice applying the modeled skill by answering a variety of questions, including constructed response and multiple choice.

> **This book is appropriate for on-grade-level students as well as for English Learners and those requiring intervention.**

Many state standards have these key expectations:	In *Conquer New Standards: Informational Text*, students will:
Students must read a "staircase" of increasingly complex texts in order to be ready for the demands of college and career-level reading.	• Read passages independently. • Encounter a range of complex passages.
Students must read challenging informational texts in a range of subjects.	• Read informational text. • Read about a wide range of subjects. • Read a variety of genres: articles, opinion essays, technical texts, speeches, biographies, autobiographies and memoirs, and more.
Students must show a "steadily growing ability" to comprehend and analyze text.	• Engage in a focused review of specific text comprehension skills. • Develop their understanding of each skill through modeled examples. • Encounter assessment items in each unit that test the unit skill as well as skills reviewed earlier in the book.
Students must respond critically to three main text types: opinion/argument, informational, and narrative.	• Read a variety of opinion/argument and informational texts and have multiple opportunities to develop responses.
Students must engage effectively in a range of collaborative discussions (one-on-one, in groups, and teacher-led) with diverse partners on appropriate topics and texts, building on others' ideas and expressing their own clearly.	• Discuss skills and engage in skill-focused activities with teachers, peers, and parents/guardians to extend their understanding of skills.
Students must use text features and specific images to clarify their understanding of a text.	• Encounter texts involving pictures, diagrams, charts, maps, and more.
Students must value evidence.	• Answer a wide array of assessment questions, both multiple choice and open ended, using evidence gathered from supplied passages to support their responses.

The companion book, *Conquer New Standards: Literary Text*, offers students opportunities to respond to literary texts.

What You'll Find in This Book

This book offers skill-specific units with appealing texts and assessment-style questions, discussion prompts to further student understanding, and activities—all of which can be used in the classroom for independent work or as homework assignments. When used as homework, the units are a great way to foster a home-school connection. The materials in this book are also great for small- and whole-group lessons. See page 11 for suggestions about how to use the units in a variety of settings.

The Units
Each unit begins with either a single text or a pair of texts.

> **Before assigning the first unit for students to do independently, model how to read—and reread—a passage.**
>
> 1. **Think about the purpose for reading the passage.**
> 2. **Read the passage all the way through to get the gist of it.**
> 3. **Reread the passage again, more slowly.**
> 4. **Refer to the passage to answer the questions.**

Target Skill
Each unit includes a target skill that students will review and practice throughout the unit.

On-Level Texts
All of the texts have been created to offer grade-appropriate reading experiences for students. Students should read the passages independently. Avoid front-loading information or pre-teaching vocabulary. This will provide students with practice similar to the assessments they will eventually take.

Unit 21

Compare/Contrast Two Texts

Misty Copeland Changes the Face of Ballet

1 Misty Copeland is changing the face of ballet in America. In the summer of 2015, Misty became the first African American principal dancer in the American Ballet Theatre (ABT). Founded in 1937 in New York City, ABT is one of the world's leading classical ballet companies. A principal holds the highest rank in a ballet company.

2 Misty started dancing at 13, at an age that is older than most professional ballerinas start. She had a tough life at home. The family struggled. They had even lived in a motel room for a while. Misty and her siblings had to sleep on the floor. Her mother didn't have a car. Misty couldn't get to ballet lessons. Thankfully, she met a ballet teacher who arranged for her to continue practicing.

3 Within three months, Misty was wearing pointe shoes. This usually takes other dancers years to achieve. As the years went on, Misty achieved many accomplishments in the world of ballet. The news of her talent spread.

4 Still, Misty faced prejudice from people who thought that only white dancers belonged in ballet. However, many more people became fans. Now Misty is trying to help other minority dancers. She is involved with Project Plié. This organization is working to bring ballet to people of all backgrounds.

94   Conquer New Standards: Informational Text • Grade 3 • © Newmark Learning, LLC

Modeling and Tips

Each unit provides a page with a brief review of the skill along with a sample question, an explanation of the sample answer, and an additional opportunity for students to apply their learning at home.

Review the Skill

This section provides a focused description of the unit's skill as a helpful reminder to students.

Home-School Connection

A Home-School Connection activity is provided in each unit. It provides a brief activity allowing parents and guardians to build on what students are learning in school. The activity is focused on the unit skill and involves everyday materials.

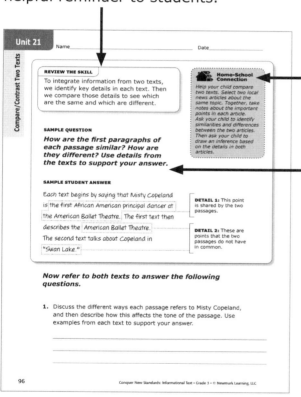

Sample Question and Sample Answer

Each unit offers a sample question focused on the unit skill followed by a sample student answer. Clues guide students to better understand how the sample answer uses text evidence to accurately and comprehensively answer the sample question. This section of each unit models how to read, answer, and provide text support with an assessment-style question, so that students are better prepared to answer questions independently.

Independent Practice

Each unit provides a variety of assessment-style questions. Students will encounter multiple-choice questions with single correct answers, multiple-choice questions with several correct answers, two-part questions, and open-ended questions requiring them to write short, constructed responses. These questions give students opportunities to apply their understanding of the unit skill and show their comprehension of the unit text. Students can work through these items independently to become experienced assessment takers.

Two-Part Questions

Multiple-Choice Questions

Constructed-Response Question

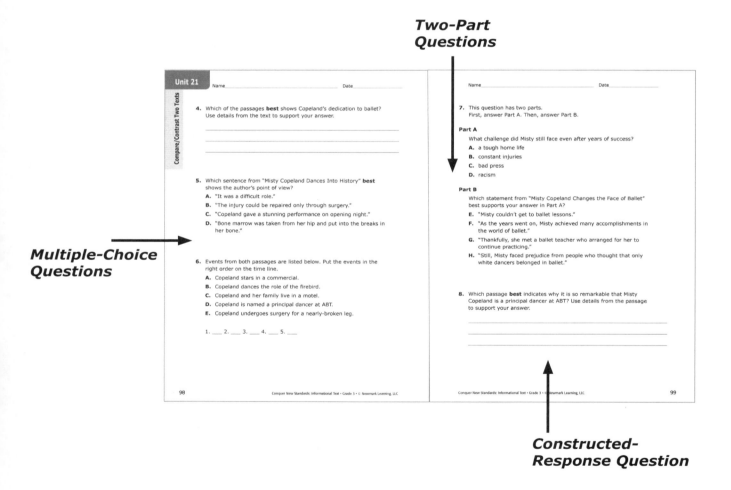

Discuss and Share

At the back of the book, you will find additional resources to support students in becoming successful readers. Sentence starters are provided for each unit to make it easy to encourage further discussion of unit texts and skills. Additional at-home activities can be used to help students and their families build greater real-world connections and a deeper understanding of the reading skills.

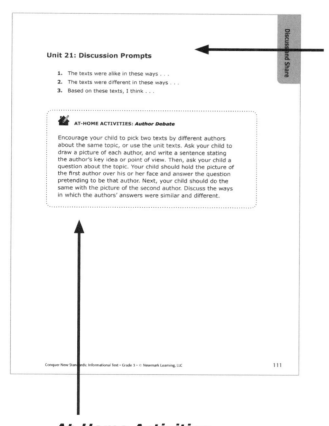

Discussion Prompts
Encourage students to talk about the skills they just reviewed. Through discussion, students can identify areas of confusion, build on each other's thoughts, and phrase skills in their own words. These prompts can be used either in the classroom, in small-group and whole-group settings, or at home to encourage a deeper consideration of important reading comprehension skills.

At-Home Activities
For each unit, there is a quick activity focused on the skill. These activities provide kinesthetic, auditory, visual, and cooperative learning experiences.

Answer Key

Each book contains an answer key that includes rationales and sample answers. Teachers may choose to:

- Review students' responses themselves.
- Assign students to review their own responses or work with a partner to review each other's responses.
- Send the answer key home so that parents or guardians can review students' responses.

Answer Key

Unit 21
pages 94–99

1. Sample answer: The first passage refers to Misty Copeland as "Misty." That makes the article seem more friendly, as if the person who wrote it knows her personally. The second passage refers to her as "Copeland." That makes the passage sound more professional and as if the author is an expert who probably does not know her personally.

2. **A** "Misty Copeland Changes the Face of Ballet" talks about the beginning of Copeland's ballet career, when she was 13. We learn about her family life and her rapid advancement as a ballerina.

3. **Part A** C

   Part B G The text says that the family "struggled." The text describes how she and her family lived in a motel, slept on the floor, and didn't have a car to get places. These details show that they were having a difficult time. These details support the idea that "struggled" must mean "had a difficult time."

4. Sample answer: "Misty Copeland Dances Into History" best shows Copeland's dedication to ballet. It talks about how much she wanted to dance the role of the firebird. She wanted it so badly that she didn't tell anyone she was hurt. The author says, "It was an injury that would have ended the career of many dancers," but Misty's career didn't end. That is dedication.

5. **C** The author could have said that Copeland performed in *The Firebird.* Instead, the author says Copeland gave "a stunning performance." "Stunning" is a positive word. It shows that the author thinks highly of Copeland.

6. (1) **C** Copeland and her family live in a motel. (2) **B** Copeland dances the role of the firebird. (3) **E** Copeland undergoes surgery for a nearly-broken leg. (4) **A** Copeland stars in a commercial. (5) **D** Copeland is named a principal dancer at ABT.

7. **Part A** D

   Part B H After achieving "many accomplishments in the world of ballet," Misty "faced prejudice from people who thought that only white dancers belonged in ballet." Prejudice is a form of racism, or thinking that one ethnic background is better than another.

8. Sample answer: The last paragraph of "Misty Copeland Changes the Face of Ballet" talks about the prejudice Copeland faced even after she achieved success. There were "people who thought that only white dancers belonged in ballet." That's why it's a big deal that she is the first African American principal dancer at ABT. She is trying to change people's understanding of ballet and how they think ballerinas should look.

Rationale

The rationale provides further explanation about the question and the unit skill, which can help students who had difficulties with a question.

Sample Answer

The sample answer provides an ideal example of a written response, which can be used to evaluate students' written responses as well as provide students with ideas for improving their written responses.

How to Use *Conquer New Standards: Informational Text*

This book has been designed so that students can work independently—either in class or at home—making it easy for you to reinforce standards mastery without sacrificing valuable teaching time. But the units also work well for small- and whole-group lessons. The chart below outlines some ideas for incorporating the units into your teaching.

If you want to use this book ENTIRELY for classroom work:		
Units	**Answer Key**	**Discuss and Share**
Assign students to work on the units independently in class.	Review students' work using the answer key, OR allow students to grade their own work with the answer key.	Use the discussion prompts to lead small-group or whole-group discussions. Use the activities as opportunities for independent, partnered, small-group, or whole-group experiences.

If you want to use this book for a COMBINATION of classroom work and homework:		
Units	**Answer Key**	**Discuss and Share**
Assign students to work on the units independently in class.	Review students' work using the answer key, OR allow students to grade their own work with the answer key.	Use the discussion prompts to lead small-group or whole-group discussions.
		Copy the activities and send home as homework opportunities for the student to complete with a parent or guardian.

If you want to use this book ENTIRELY for homework:		
Units	**Answer Key**	**Discuss and Share**
Copy the Parent/Guardian Letter and units and send home for students to do as homework.	Copy the answer key for students, parents, or guardians to use to review the students' work.	Copy the discussion prompts and activities to send home as homework, encouraging parent/guardian involvement.

Dear Parent or Guardian,

This year, your child will be completing informational text units for homework. The goal of these units is to ensure that your child has the skills necessary to comprehend a variety of key informational text types, such as articles, speeches, biographies, and technical texts.

There are three parts in the take-home unit:
1) the informational text passage
2) a review of the skill being addressed that includes a sample question and sample answer about the text
3) questions about the passage for your child to answer

Encourage your child to read each passage independently if possible, and then review the skill and the sample question and answer. Finally, have him or her answer the unit questions.

The unit also includes engaging activities for you to do with your child at home to further support his or her understanding.

We hope you'll agree that the skills practice that *Conquer New Standards: Informational Text* offers will not only help your child to become a better reader, but also provide him or her with the support needed to become a more successful student.

Estimados padres o tutores:

La tarea de su hija(o) para este año consiste en leer y practicar ejercicios de unidades de textos informativos. El objetivo de estas unidades es garantizar que su hija(o) posea las destrezas necesarias para entender una amplia variedad de textos informativos como artículos, discursos, biografías y textos técnicos.

La unidad de la tarea en casa consta de tres partes:
1) el pasaje de texto informativo
2) un repaso de la destreza a desarrollar, que incluye ejemplos de pregunta y respuesta sobre el texto
3) preguntas acerca del pasaje para que su hija(o) las responda

Anime a su hija(o) a leer cada pasaje de manera independiente, si es posible. Después, repase la destreza y los ejemplos de pregunta y respuesta. Para terminar, pídale que responda las preguntas de la unidad.

La unidad también incluye entretenidas actividades para que las hagan juntos en casa. Esto apoyará aún más la habilidad de comprensión de su hija(o).

Confiamos en que estará de acuerdo que la práctica de destrezas que ofrece *Conquer New Standards: Informational Text,* ayudará a su hija(o) a ser mejor lector(a) y, además, le brinda el apoyo necesario para ser un(a) estudiante de éxito.

Roosevelt's Freedoms

1   In 1941, U.S. president Franklin Delano Roosevelt gave his famous Four Freedoms speech. In it, he proposed four basic human rights. He wanted people everywhere in the world to enjoy them.

2   At the time, European countries were fighting in a war. Great Britain asked for help from the United States. Great Britain was fighting against Germany. But many U.S. citizens were against this idea. They wanted to stay out of world problems, especially since World War I had taken so many lives. So Roosevelt made his case before Congress to change their minds.

3   He outlined the following freedoms:

4   Freedom of speech: the right to freely communicate opinions and ideas.

5   Freedom of worship: the right to practice any religion, or to not practice any religion at all.

6   Freedom from want: the right to have all the food, housing, and shelter one needs.

7   Freedom from fear: the right to feel safe and secure as nations try to promote peace.

8   The United States no longer stayed neutral after his speech. The citizens supported Roosevelt. Within months, the United States joined the war effort. And ever since then, people have called on Roosevelt's words to promote freedom throughout the world.

Conquer New Standards: Informational Text • Grade 3 • © Newmark Learning, LLC

To answer questions about a text, we can think about what the question is asking. Then we can look back at the text for details that tell us the answer.

Home-School Connection

Help your child understand that details in a text can help answer questions he or she may have about the text. After reading the text, ask your child questions, such as "Whom is this text about? What happened? Where? When? Why?" and "How?" Then encourage your child to find details in the text that answer these questions.

SAMPLE QUESTION

What does the Four Freedoms speech say about free speech? Use details from the article to support your response.

SAMPLE STUDENT ANSWER

The Four Freedoms speech says that people should have the freedom of speech. The text says "the right to freely communicate opinions and ideas."

ANSWER: This answers the question.

DETAIL: This provides details from the text to support the answer.

Now refer to "Roosevelt's Freedoms" to answer the following questions.

1. Describe what was happening in the world when Roosevelt gave his speech. Use examples from the article to support your response.

_____

_____

_____

2. What are the Four Freedoms? Use details from the article to support your answer.

_____

_____

_____

3. Which ideas are **not** part of the Four Freedoms? Select **two.**

   A. right to be safe

   B. right to make war

   C. right to have food

   D. right to have shelter

   E. right to have opinions

   F. right to practice medicine

4. Look at the cause-and-effect box.

Cause	Effect
Roosevelt gave the Four Freedoms speech.	

Which detail from the passage goes in the "effect" box?

   A. "Great Britain asked for help."

   B. "Within months, the United States joined the war effort."

   C. "But many U.S. citizens were against this idea."

   D. "European countries were fighting in a war."

5. Who should be able to have the Four Freedoms according to Roosevelt?

   A. Congress

   B. Europeans

   C. everyone

   D. Germans

6. This has question two parts.

First answer Part A. Then answer Part B.

Part A

What is the meaning of the word "communicate" in paragraph 4?

   A. eat

   B. live

   C. talk

   D. think

Part B

What details give a clue to the meaning of "communicate"?

   E. "European countries were fighting"

   F. "the right to have all the food"

   G. "try to promote peace"

   H. "Freedom of speech"

Adapted and excerpted from

The Four Freedoms

A speech given by Franklin Delano Roosevelt on January 6, 1941

1   The basic things expected by our people are simple. They are: equality of opportunity for youth and for others, jobs for those who can work, security for those who need it, the ending of special privilege for the few, the preservation of civil liberties for all, and the enjoyment of the fruits of scientific progress. . . .

2   We should bring more citizens under the coverage of old-age pensions and unemployment insurance. We should widen the opportunity for medical care. We should plan a better system by which people deserving or needing employment may obtain it.

3   In the future days, we look forward to a world founded upon four essential human freedoms.

4   The first is freedom of speech and expression—everywhere in the world. The second is freedom of every person to worship in his own way—everywhere in the world. The third is freedom from want. This means that every nation can have a healthy peacetime life—everywhere in the world. The fourth is freedom from fear. This means reducing weapons worldwide so that no nation will be able to commit an act of physical aggression against any neighbor—anywhere in the world.

5   That is no vision of a distant time. It is a definite basis for a kind of world in our own time and generation.

6   Freedom means the supremacy of human rights everywhere. Our support goes to those who struggle to gain those rights and keep them. Our strength is our unity of purpose.

REVIEW THE SKILL

To understand an article, we ask questions about it. Then we go back to the text to find details that answer our questions.

SAMPLE QUESTION

Who should have the rights described in the Four Freedoms? Use details from the text to support your answer.

SAMPLE STUDENT ANSWER

The Four Freedoms are meant for everybody. Roosevelt repeats the word "world" many times. He also says words such as "everywhere." He does not mention one specific country. So everyone everywhere should have these rights.

CLUE 1: This word tells us whom Roosevelt is including when he talks about the Four Freedoms.

CLUE 2: "Everywhere" tells us that Roosevelt is not speaking about one specific country.

Now refer to "The Four Freedoms" to answer the following questions.

1. Describe three basic things that Roosevelt wants for all people. Use details from the speech to support your answer.

    _____

    _____

    _____

2. Which sentence **best** describes how Roosevelt feels about the Four Freedoms?

   A. Everyone already has all these basic rights.

   B. Basic rights are complicated and not very simple.

   C. Basic rights are most important for young people.

   D. We should support people working to get their basic rights.

3. This question has two parts.

First answer Part A. Then answer Part B.

Part A

What is the meaning of the word "struggle" as it is used in paragraph 6?

   A. ask for

   B. fight for

   C. hope for

   D. return to

Part B

Which details are clues to the meaning of "struggle"? Select **two.**

   E. "freedom"

   F. "gain"

   G. "keep"

   H. "rights"

   I. "unity"

4. According to Roosevelt, what should happen to the "special privilege for the few"? Use details from the text to support your answer.

_____

_____

_____

5. Which details below **best** support the idea that Roosevelt thought people in 1941 should have these basic rights? Choose **two.**

   A. "for a kind of world in our own time and generation"

   B. "In the future days, we look forward to a world"

   C. "Our strength is our unity of purpose."

   D. "That is no vision of a distant time."

   E. "We should plan a better system"

Who Was Sally Ride?

1   Sally Ride was the first American woman to fly in space. For fun, she liked to run. She also played tennis, volleyball, and softball. Ride wrote science books for children. The books are about exploring space.

2   Ride was born on May 26, 1951, in California. After high school, she went to Stanford University in California. She earned degrees in physics. Physics is a type of science.

3   NASA began looking for female astronauts in 1977. Ride was a student then. She saw an ad from NASA in a newspaper. It invited women to apply to the astronaut program. Ride applied for the job. She was one of six women picked!

4   On June 18, 1983, Ride became the first American woman to fly in space. She was an astronaut on a space shuttle mission. Her job was to work the robotic arm. She used the arm to help put satellites into space. She flew on the space shuttle again in 1984.

5   Ride stopped working for NASA in 1987. She started teaching at the University of California in San Diego. She looked for ways to help women and girls who wanted to study science and math. She came up with a special project. It lets students take pictures of Earth using a camera on the International Space Station.

6   In 2003, Ride was added to the Astronaut Hall of Fame. This honors astronauts for their hard work.

7   Until her death on July 23, 2012, Ride continued to help students study science and math. She wrote science books for students and teachers. She worked with science programs and festivals around the United States.

REVIEW THE SKILL

The main idea of a text is the most important idea or message expressed by the text. Look at the details and identify what message the details express.

SAMPLE QUESTION

Why was Sally Ride an important person? Use details from the text to support your answer.

SAMPLE STUDENT ANSWER

Sally Ride was the first American woman to fly into space. The text said in June 1983, Ride "became the first American woman to fly in space." She was also "added to the Astronaut Hall of Fame" in 2003.

ANSWER: This statement answers the question.

CLUE: These details show why Sally Ride was an important American astronaut.

Now refer to "Who Was Sally Ride?" to answer the following questions.

1. Describe Sally Ride's job on the space shuttle. Use details from the text to support your answer.

_____

_____

_____

2. How did Sally Ride become the first American woman to fly in space?

   A. Ride stopped working for NASA in 1987.

   B. She had always wanted to be an astronaut.

   C. She saw an ad looking for astronauts and applied for the job.

   D. She started teaching at the University of California in San Diego.

3. This question has two parts.

First answer Part A. Then answer Part B.

Part A

In paragraph 6, what is the meaning of the word "honors"?

   A. announces

   B. gives

   C. recognizes

   D. takes

Part B

What detail gives a clue to the meaning of "honors"?

   E. "hard work"

   F. "was added"

   G. "Hall of Fame"

   H. "honors astronauts"

4. Look at the cause-and-effect box.

Cause	Effect
Sally Ride was the first American woman to travel to space.	

Which of the following goes in the "effect" box?

A. Sally Ride studied science.

B. Sally Ride liked to play sports.

C. She was added to the Astronaut Hall of Fame.

D. She wrote science books for students and teachers.

5. Put the events below in the right order.

A. She came up with a project involving a special camera.

B. In 1983, she was the first American woman to fly in space.

C. She flew on the space shuttle again in 1984.

D. She stopped working for NASA in 1987.

E. She saw a NASA ad in the newspaper.

F. She earned degrees in physics.

1. ____ 2. ____ 3. ____ 4. ____ 5. ____ 6. ____

6. Besides traveling into space, how else did Sally Ride get involved with science? Use details from the text to support your answer.

_____

_____

_____

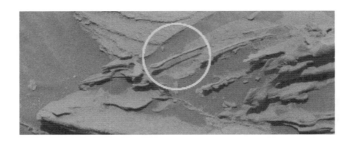

Rocking Out on Mars

1 So there's a floating spoon on Mars. (Wait! What? Is there a fork and knife, too? Do Martians prefer spoons?)

2 We'll put the question of the Red Planet's preferred utensils aside for the moment. Now, let's look at how Earthlings saw this floating spoon in the first place. And for that matter, how we saw rats, iguanas, and elephants too.

3 Since 2012, the Curiosity rover has been creeping along Mars's surface. The rover is the size of a car. It has a seven-foot-long arm, which can snap pictures with an advanced camera. NASA beams these images back to Earth.

4 Scientists wanted to know whether Mars can support life. So far, scientists have found only rocks. Lots and lots of rocks.

5 The floating spoon that was seen in one of these photos is actually just a rock that is shaped like a floating spoon. This is also true of all those other shapes!

6 Even though there is no real spoon on Mars, still, this special rock tells us about geology on Mars. On Earth, wind erosion has made some awesome shapes. Wind has been known to carve arches and towers out of rocks. These things look man-made, but actually the wind made them.

7 On Mars, the process of shaping rocks is similar. Scientists think the constant, round-the-clock wind on Mars produced these amazing shapes.

8 As Curiosity continues its mission, we'll see more fascinating images. So hold onto your spoons and forks (or sporks!). There's going to be a lot to chew on.

Conquer New Standards: Informational Text • Grade 3 • © Newmark Learning, LLC

Name_____ Date_____

Home-School Connection

Read your child a short news article or watch a short news broadcast. Ask your child to draw two circles. In one circle, your child should write the most important ideas and details. The less important ideas and details should be written in the second circle. Then ask, "Why are these important? Why are those less important?"

SAMPLE QUESTION

How do we know about the rock formations on Mars? Use details from the text to support your answer.

SAMPLE STUDENT ANSWER

We know about the rock formations on Mars because of the Curiosity rover. It moves along Mars's surface and takes pictures with its long arm. NASA sends these pictures to Earth.

DETAIL 1: These details tell how the rock formations were discovered.

DETAIL 2: This detail tells who is in charge of the exploration on Mars.

Now refer to "Rocking Out on Mars" to answer the following questions.

1. What has been discovered on Mars? Use details from the text to support your answer.

_____

_____

_____

Name_____ Date_____

2. Read this paragraph from the text again.

    "Scientists wanted to know whether Mars can support
    life. So far, scientists have found only rocks. Lots and lots
    of rocks."

    Which detail shows that scientists do not believe there is life
    on Mars?

    A. "lots and lots"

    B. "found only rocks"

    C. "Mars can support life."

    D. "Scientists wanted to know"

3. Which of the following is a key idea in the text?

    A. that there is no life on Mars

    B. that Martians might prefer spoons

    C. that shapes on Mars are made with wind

    D. that rocks on Mars are smaller than rocks on Earth

4. What is a key idea in paragraph 6? Use details from the text to
    support your answer.

    _____

    _____

    _____

5. This question has two parts.

First answer Part A. Then answer Part B.

Part A

In paragraph 7, what is the meaning of the word "constant"?

    A. nonstop

    B. old

    C. strong

    D. weak

Part B

What detail from the text **best** supports your answer to Part A?

    E. "amazing"

    F. "carve"

    G. "erosion"

    H. "round-the-clock"

6. Which detail **best** supports the key idea that NASA found rocks in different shapes on Mars? Choose **two**.

    A. "This is also true of all those other shapes!"

    B. "how we saw rats, iguanas, and elephants too"

    C. "this special rock tells us about geology on Mars"

    D. "which can snap pictures with an advanced camera"

    E. "The floating spoon that was seen in one of these photos"

Table Manners

1   You probably have learned rules about how to eat. Maybe you learned to eat with a fork and not with your hands. Or maybe you put a napkin on your lap. These rules for how we eat are called table manners.

2   Around the world, there are different rules for how to eat. People in different countries have different table manners. Pick a country anywhere in the world to dine in. Here's what you might expect:

3   Consider this. In Egypt, a chef could be insulted if a person uses salt. This might suggest that you think the food is bland.

4   You might get a half cup of tea in Kazakhstan. This is if the host wants you to stay. You'll get a full cup if the host wants you to leave.

5   In India, you should not leave the table until your host has finished eating.

6   In France, an empty plate means you enjoyed the meal. But in the Philippines, don't finish all your food. It suggests that your host has not fed you enough.

7   Never eat with your hands in Chile. It's offensive and rude! Always use utensils. Forks, spoons, and knives only.

8   If you want to appear fancy in Britain, sip only from the side of your spoon. In Thailand, use your fork only to put food into a spoon. Never use a fork itself to eat.

9   Take care with chopsticks in China and Japan. Don't point them in China. And don't pass food with them in Japan.

10 All of these differences show the same thing. Each culture has its own way to eat its food.

Conquer New Standards: Informational Text • Grade 3 • © Newmark Learning, LLC

REVIEW THE SKILL

Details can be names of people or places, descriptions of things, and more. Supporting details are those details that support an idea in the text.

 Home-School Connection

Help your child develop the skill of identifying supporting details. After each paragraph in the text, pause and share an opinion you have about the table manners described. Ask your child to identify any details in what you just read that support your opinion.

SAMPLE QUESTION

Table manners in France and the Philippines are different. What details from the passage support this idea?

SAMPLE STUDENT ANSWER

Table manners in France and the Philippines are different. For example, in France, finishing the food on your plate means you were happy with your meal. But in the Philippines, if you finish the food on your plate, it means you are unhappy because you were not fed enough.

CLUE 1: The answer contains lots of supporting details. This detail shows table manners in France.

CLUE 2: This detail shows table manners in the Philippines. Overall, the details in this answer support the idea that table manners are different in France and the Philippines.

Now refer to "Table Manners" to answer the questions.

1. What is a table manner that is the same in two different countries? Use details from the text to support your answer.

_____

_____

_____

2. Which of the following details **best** supports the idea that people in many places follow rules when they eat?

   A. "Around the world, there are different rules for how to eat."

   B. "You probably have learned rules about how to eat."

   C. "You might get a half cup of tea in Kazakhstan."

   D. "All of these differences show the same thing."

3. This question has two parts.

   First answer Part A. Then answer Part B.

Part A

In paragraph 7, what is the meaning of the word "offensive"?

   A. very nice

   B. not polite

   C. too hungry

   D. very friendly

Part B

What detail from the passage **best** supports your answer in Part A?

   E. "enjoyed"

   F. "fancy"

   G. "rude"

   H. "utensils"

4. Many countries have rules about how to use utensils. Pick **three** countries that have rules about using utensils.

    A. Britain

    B. Chile

    C. France

    D. Egypt

    E. Kazakhstan

    F. Thailand

5. Which sentence from the passage **best** supports the idea that people throughout the world have unique table manners?

    A. "Take care with chopsticks in China and Japan."

    B. "Never eat with your hands in Chile."

    C. "People in different countries have different table manners."

    D. "Maybe you learned to eat with a fork and not with your hands."

6. In Egypt, how would you show respect to the person who cooked food for you? Use details from the passage to support your answer.

_____

_____

_____

The Tale of the Tooth Mouse

1   Around the world, some children believe in tooth fairies that take their baby teeth and leave presents behind. In other countries, children believe in tooth mice. And some believe in beings that are . . . both.

2   The legend of the Tooth Fairy has been told for ages in the United States. But what does she look like? What does she do with those teeth? Nobody really agrees.

3   In Spain and in Latin American countries, a little mouse comes scurrying. And like our fairy, El Ratoncito Perez leaves coins and other presents behind. Luis Coloma created this character in 1894. In his story, Perez wore a tiny straw hat, gold eyeglasses, and a red satchel on his shoulder.

4   The story says that, one night, Perez went to visit the young King Bubi, whose tooth had just fallen out. The king was still a young child. Perez put the tip of his tail in the king's nostril and changed Bubi into a mouse! Then Perez and Bubi traveled through the drains of the city together. Bubi saw many poor children that Perez helped. His heart softened. Back in his bedroom, Bubi became a child again. And he grew up to be a generous king.

5   In France, there's a different spin, La Petite Souris—the fairy that turns into a mouse! Based on a 17th-century tale, this fairy mouse wanted to save a queen from an evil king. So she hid under the king's pillow and knocked out all his teeth.

6   Traditionally, these stories are told to make kids feel better about losing teeth. Whether it's a fairy or a mouse that leaves them presents depends on where they wake up.

Name_____ Date_____

REVIEW THE SKILL

Informational texts can be organized in many ways. Details can be in time order (sequential), grouped by cause and effect, compare and contrast, or other ways.

Home-School Connection

Help your child practice identifying relationships in informational texts. Show your child two types of informational texts, such as an instruction manual and a news article. Read through each document together. Look for clue words that show relationships, such as "first," "next," "because," and "therefore."

SAMPLE QUESTION

How do legends about teeth differ around the world? Use details from the text to support your answer.

SAMPLE STUDENT ANSWER

In some parts of the word, children are told about the Tooth Fairy. In other parts of the world, children learn about mice who take teeth.

DETAIL 1: This detail tells what children in some parts of the world believe.

DETAIL 2: This detail tells how children believe differently in other places.

Now refer to "The Tale of The Tooth Mouse" to answer the following questions.

1. How did the idea of El Ratoncito Perez, the tooth mouse, begin? Use details from the text to support your answer.

_____

_____

_____

2. Which of the following **best** describes how the passage is structured?

    A. time order

    B. compare and contrast

    C. cause and effect

    D. problem and solution

3. How did Perez change King Bubi?

    A. He made him rich.

    B. He made him poor.

    C. He turned him into a mouse.

    D. He turned him into the Tooth Fairy.

4. Events from Luis Coloma's story are listed below. Put the events in the right order on the time line.

    A. Perez and Bubi traveled through the drains of the city.

    B. Perez visited King Bubi in the middle of the night.

    C. Perez put the tip of his tail in Bubi's nostril.

    D. Bubi grew up and became very generous.

    E. Bubi saw many poor children.

    1. ____ 2. ____ 3. ____ 4. ____ 5. ____

5. This has question two parts.

First answer Part A. Then answer Part B.

Part A

Which word is a **synonym** for the word "spin" in paragraph 5?

A. reason

B. round

C. twirl

D. version

Part B

Which of the following statements **best** supports your answer in Part A?

E. The paragraph tells a similar but different story.

F. The paragraph explains details about the story.

G. The paragraph repeats the same story again.

H. The paragraph is very long.

6. Why are these stories about teeth told to children? Use details from the text to support your answer.

_____

_____

_____

Bell Rings Twice

1 On January 25, 1915, Alexander Graham Bell sat in New York and picked up a phone. Into it he said, "Mr. Watson, come here. I want you." In seconds, his voice traveled 3,400 miles. It went all the way to San Francisco.

2 Across the nation, Thomas A. Watson replied, "It will take me five days to get there now!"

3 Joking aside, this was a very important event. Bell had just made one of the first official transcontinental phone calls. His greeting recalled another historic moment. Together, Bell and Watson had spent several years experimenting with sending sound across wires. Watson had been Bell's assistant. The two men made the first telephone call on March 10, 1876. That time, Bell was only a room away from Watson. He spoke those same words.

4 In those beginning years, early telephone calls could happen only across short distances. Bell and others kept working to improve the telephone's range. Bell promoted his invention at public events. At each demonstration, the distance between phones was greater.

5 Bell eventually moved onto other experiments. The telephone company AT&T continued working to connect calls across the country. It was difficult because a voice signal would naturally weaken as it traveled long distances. Then AT&T found a way to strengthen voice signals.

6 It was called the Audion. Invented by Lee De Forest, it was a vacuum tube device that was placed on telephone wires from coast to coast. Every time a voice hit an Audion, its signal was boosted.

7 Bell and Watson were chosen to make the first transcontinental call in 1915. For the second time in history, their words rang loudly.

Conquer New Standards: Informational Text • Grade 3 • © Newmark Learning, LLC

REVIEW THE SKILL

Historical texts provide details about events from history. These details might be organized in time order, by cause/effect, by problem/solution, or by compare/contrast.

 Home-School Connection

Help your child describe the relationships between events. Ask your child to recall an important day in his or her life. Then, ask your child to write a list of all the details he or she remembers about this day. Working together, order the details in different ways, such as in sequential order, presenting a problem and then a solution, etc.

SAMPLE QUESTION

How do we know that Alexander Graham Bell's 1915 phone call was an important moment? Use details from the text in your answer.

SAMPLE STUDENT ANSWER

The author says "Joking aside, this was a very important event." It was one of the first times that a human voice traveled more than 3,000 miles. It was one of the first calls made from one coast of the United States to the other.

DETAIL 1: This quote from the text tells us how important the event was.

DETAIL 2: The words "first times" signal that a breakthrough had been made. That's important.

Now refer to "Bell Rings Twice" to answer the questions.

1. Describe the relationship between Bell and Watson. Use details from the text to support your answer.

_____

_____

_____

Name_____ Date_____

2. In the early years, why were telephone calls made only across short distances?

   A. because voice signals weakened over distances

   B. because a vacuum tube made the voices quiet

   C. because the telephone wires were too short

   D. because not everyone had a phone

3. Look at the cause-and-effect box.

Cause	Effect
	Bell called Watson from the next room.

Which detail from the passage goes in the "cause" box?

   A. "The two men made the first telephone call on March 10, 1876."

   B. "Alexander Graham Bell sat in New York and picked up a phone."

   C. "Bell had just made one of the first official transcontinental phone calls."

   D. "Together Bell and Watson had spent several years experimenting with sending sound across wires."

4. Describe the significance of Bell and Watson's joke. Use details from the text to support your answer.

_____

_____

_____

Conquer New Standards: Informational Text • Grade 3 • © Newmark Learning, LLC

5. This has question two parts.

First answer Part A. Then answer Part B.

Part A

In the fourth paragraph, what is the meaning of the word "range"?

A. the distance something can travel

B. a distant, faraway part of the country

C. a hot part of a stove on which to cook

D. a large field or area to play on

Part B

Which of the following details **best** supports your answer to Part A?

E. "a vacuum tube device that was placed on telephone wires from coast to coast"

F. "telephone calls could happen only across short distances"

G. "Bell and Watson had spent several years experimenting"

H. "Bell promoted his invention at public events."

6. Events from "Bell Rings Twice" are listed below. Put the events in the correct order on the time line.

A. Alexander Graham Bell called Thomas A. Watson in California.

B. AT&T put Audions on telephone wires from coast to coast.

C. AT&T found a device to strengthen voice signals.

D. Alexander Graham Bell invented the telephone.

E. Lee de Forest invented the Audion.

1. ____ 2. ____ 3. ____ 4. ____ 5. ____

The Big World of Microbes

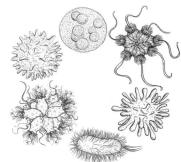

1   Can you picture a microbe—one of the universe's tiniest creatures?

2   Think of a small animal. Let's say a hamster. No, they're too big. What about a ladybug? No, much too big. A flea, you might say. Still WAY too big!

3   Microbes are microscopic. They can be seen only with a microscope. Seeing a microbe with the naked eye would be like sucking an elephant through a straw. It's impossible!

4   Microbes are also known as germs. They are the bacteria or viruses that get people sick. When someone sneezes, invisible microbes fly into the air. Without knowing it, another person can easily inhale these germs.

5   The molds on fruit and bread are other types of microbes. The fungi that grow on trees and create mushrooms are microbes. So you may wonder, if mold is so small, why can I see it on bread? And why can I see it on mushrooms? That's because even a tiny speck of mold or fungus is actually a colony of microbes. It takes millions upon millions of microbes to make a colony, or group.

6   Every living thing in the world is covered with microbes. Trillions and trillions and trillions of them. It's a good thing that most microbes help us. Humans have them inside their stomachs. They help break down food. They also live all over the skin. Many microbes actually fight off bad germs and keep people from getting sick.

7   Certain microbes help Earth's natural environments. They break down dead plants, animal waste, and human garbage. This process cleans our oceans and forests.

8   It might be difficult to see these tiny creatures. But it's easy to see the BIG job they do.

Scientific texts provide details about scientific topics. These details might be organized in time order, by cause/effect, by problem/solution, or by compare/contrast.

SAMPLE QUESTION

How are microbes different from hamsters, ladybugs, or fleas? Use details from the text in your answer.

SAMPLE STUDENT ANSWER

Microbes are much smaller than these other living things. Those living things are "WAY too big!" Microbes are so tiny that it takes millions of microbes to create something that can been seen by the naked eye.

CLUE 1: This sentence compares microbes with the other living things.

CLUE 2: This detail describes exactly how tiny microbes are.

Now refer to "The Big World of Microbes" to answer the following questions.

1. How does the size of germs contribute to people getting sick? Use details from the text to support your answer.

_____

_____

_____

2. When you look at a speck of mold, how many microbes are you **most likely** seeing?

   A. a million or more

   B. about 100,000

   C. about 10,000

   D. about 1,000

3. Which of the following are **synonyms** for the word "colony" in paragraph 5? Choose **two.**

   A. animal

   B. group

   C. mushroom

   D. space

   E. team

4. Which of the following **best** describes how paragraphs 1–3 are structured?

   A. time order

   B. cause and effect

   C. compare and contrast

   D. problem and solution

5. Look at the cause-and-effect box.

Cause	Effect
	A person inhales germs.

Which of the following goes in the "cause" box?

   A. Someone sneezes and sends microbes into the air.

   B. Humans have microbes inside their stomachs.

   C. Someone sucks microbes through a straw.

   D. Microbes fight off bad germs.

6. This has question two parts.

   First answer Part A. Then answer Part B.

Part A

What role do microbes have in our forests and oceans?

   A. Microbes help to destroy our forests and oceans.

   B. Microbes help to clean our forests and oceans.

   C. Microbes make our forests and oceans bigger.

   D. Microbes clog our forests and oceans.

Part B

Which details from the passage **best** support your answer in Part A? Choose **two.**

   E. "The fungi that grow on trees and create mushrooms are microbes."

   F. "They break down dead plants, animal waste, and human garbage."

   G. "Every living thing in the world is covered with microbes."

   H. "Many microbes actually fight off bad germs."

   I. "This process cleans our oceans and forests."

How to Grow Tulips

1   You can have colorful friends visit you every spring: tulips! They are perennial flowers. They will grow back every year. Follow these steps to bring these beauties into your life.

2   **Step 1:** Tulip bulbs should be planted in the fall. Plant them 6 to 8 weeks before the first hard frost. A farmer's almanac can help you determine when to expect frost.

3   **Step 2:** Plant bulbs in a sunny spot. Choose a place that gets full or afternoon sun every day. Tulips don't like too much moisture. Well-drained soils work best. You can also mix sand into your soil to help with drainage.

4   **Step 3:** Space bulbs 4–6 inches apart on the ground. Dig an 8-inch-deep hole for each bulb.

5   **Step 4:** Place a bulb in each hole with the pointy end facing up. Cover with soil. Press the soil firmly.

6   **Step 5:** Water bulbs only after you plant them. Bulbs don't like "wet feet." Bulbs need water only to start growth. Then leave them alone. Never water bulb beds. That could cause rot.

7   **Step 6:** Use compost or another organic fertilizer to feed them.

8   **Step 7:** Then, wait! The days will start to slowly get brighter and warmer. The trees will fill with green. And presto, you'll have tulips year after year!

> **Tip for a long vase life:**
> Cut tulip stems diagonally. Wrap the top part of the stems in a funnel of newspaper. Stand them in cool water for an hour or two. Then re-cut the stems. Your cut tulips should last one week.

Technical texts are often arranged in numbered steps. The order of these steps tells us what should happen first, next, and last.

SAMPLE QUESTION

When is the best time to plant tulips? Use details from the text to support your answer.

SAMPLE STUDENT ANSWER

Tulips should be planted in the fall. The text says they should be planted "6 to 8 weeks" before frost covers the ground.

DETAIL 1: This detail tells the best season to plant tulips in.

DETAIL 2: This detail tells exactly when to plant tulips.

Now refer to "How to Grow Tulips" to answer the questions.

1. Where should tulip bulbs be planted? Use details from the text to support your answer.

_____

_____

_____

2. Steps from the passage are listed below. Arrange the steps in the correct order.

   A. "Place a bulb in each hole with the pointy end facing up."

   B. "Space bulbs 4–6 inches apart on the ground."

   C. "Dig an 8-inch-deep hole for each bulb."

   D. "Press the soil firmly."

   E. "Cover with soil."

   1. ____ 2. ____ 3. ____ 4. ____ 5. ____

3. What happens if you water bulb beds?

   A. The bulbs will grow upside down.

   B. The bulbs will multiply.

   C. The bulbs will rot.

   D. The bulbs will die.

4. What should newly planted bulbs be fed?

   A. worms

   B. tulip leaves

   C. cedar shavings

   D. compost or organic fertilizer

5. This has question two parts.

First answer Part A. Then answer Part B.

Part A

What is the meaning of the word "perennial" in paragraph 1?

  A. grows red

  B. returns yearly

  C. dies after one season

  D. continues to bloom in winter

Part B

Which words or phrases from the text give a clue to the meaning of "perennial"? Choose **two.**

  E. "every spring"

  F. "then leave them alone"

  G. "year after year"

  H. "mix sand"

6. How can you make tulips last longer? Put the steps in the correct order. Use details from the text to support your answer.

_____

_____

_____

The White House Kitchen Garden

1   The White House Kitchen Garden is home to many leafy greens, herbs, and berries. It provides fresh foods for the First Family to enjoy each day. On March 20, 2009, students from Washington's Bancroft Elementary School and First Lady Michelle Obama broke ground on the vegetable garden. It was the first one at the White House since World War II.

2   Today, the garden is planted, tended, and harvested by Mrs. Obama, White House staff, and the National Park Service. Tours of the garden are available to schools and community groups.

3   How does the White House Kitchen Garden grow? Just like any other garden! It needs plenty of sunshine and nurturing. It also needs the right amount of water. It needs proper soiling methods too.

4   In response to the First Lady's passion for healthy eating, people across the country have started vegetable gardens at home. Growing your own fruits and vegetables is a great way to learn where food comes from. It's a way to spend time with others. It helps you include healthy foods in your favorite meals.

5   Even if you don't consider yourself a "master gardener," you can harvest your own produce. You can do this at school or in your backyard. You can do this around your community.

Name_____ Date_____

As you read, identify unfamiliar words. Use context clues to understand these words. A context clue is a nearby word or phrase that hints at the unknown word's meaning.

Home-School Connection

Help your child decode unknown vocabulary words. Make a small booklet out of letter-sized paper, about five pages or so. Encourage your child to record unfamiliar words from the passage on each page. Then your child can show the meaning of each word by drawing pictures or gluing magazine clippings.

SAMPLE QUESTION

What does the word "greens" mean as it is used in paragraph 1? Use details from the text to support your answer.

SAMPLE STUDENT ANSWER

"Greens" are vegetables, such as spinach and lettuce. First, I looked at the title, "The White House Kitchen Garden." It made me think about foods that grow in gardens. Then I looked at the word "leafy." Spinach and lettuce are green, leafy things that grow in gardens.

CLUE 1: The article's title hints at the answer.

CLUE 2: This detail describes the greens. This is a context clue. We can make an inference based on it.

Now refer to "The White House Kitchen Garden" to answer the following questions.

1. What does the phrase "broke ground" mean as it is used in paragraph 1? Use details from the passage to support your answer.

_____

_____

_____

2. What is the meaning of "tended" as it is used in paragraph 2?

   A. cleaned up

   B. cooked with

   C. taken care of

   D. watched closely

3. What does the word "proper" suggest as it is used in paragraph 3?
   Choose **two** answers.

   A. Gardens don't take a lot of thought to care for.

   B. There is a correct way of handling the soil.

   C. There is a better way to garden.

   D. Gardens shouldn't be watered.

   E. Soil needs special care.

4. Look at the cause-and-effect box.

Cause	Effect
The First Lady planted a fruit and vegetable garden at the White House.	

Which detail from the passage goes in the "effect" box?

   A. There was a garden at the White House during World War II.

   B. People across the country are now growing gardens.

   C. First Lady Michelle Obama visited an elementary school.

   D. There are more gardens at national parks.

5. This has question two parts.

First answer Part A. Then answer Part B.

Part A

Reread this phrase from paragraph 5.

"Even if you don't consider yourself a 'master gardener'"

What idea does the author suggest with this phrase?

A. Some people are experts at gardening, but you don't have to be.

B. Some people eat healthier foods than other people.

C. Only experts should try to grow their own food.

D. Gardening is enjoyable for everyone.

Part B

Which of the following statements **best** supports your answer in Part A?

E. Gardens take a lot of work.

F. You need to take gardening classes.

G. You can visit the White House garden.

H. You can grow a garden at home or in your community.

6. Why should people grow their own gardens? Use details from the text to support your answer.

_____

_____

_____

The Very First Labor Day: September 5, 1882

1   If you could create a holiday, what would it be called? What date would you choose? Peter J. McGuire, a carpenter and labor union leader, was the person who came up with the idea for Labor Day. He thought American workers should be honored with their own day. He proposed his idea to New York's Central Labor Union early in 1882. The other workers thought the holiday was a good idea, too.

2   There were four long months between Independence Day and Thanksgiving when American workers didn't have time off for any national holidays. So Peter suggested a month halfway in between. But what date should they choose?

3   The very first Labor Day was held on Tuesday, September 5, 1882. It was held in New York City. The day was celebrated with a picnic, concert, and speeches. Ten thousand workers marched in a parade from City Hall to a popular place called Union Square.

4   Soon after that first celebration, the holiday was moved to the first Monday in September, the day we still honor. Congress passed legislation making Labor Day a national holiday in 1894. Labor Day is not just a day to celebrate the accomplishments of workers. For some people, it is also a day to talk about their concerns and to discuss ways to get better working conditions and salaries. How do you celebrate the last holiday of the summer?

Independence Day is on July 4. It is also known as the Fourth of July. On this day, we remember when the United States was first formed. Thanksgiving is in November. It is always on the fourth Thursday of the month. It is a day for giving thanks.

REVIEW THE SKILL

You may find unfamiliar words while reading social studies or history texts. Use clues in the text, like words or phrases, that hint at the unfamiliar word's meaning. Also think about the subject you're reading about. Use what you already know about that subject to help you understand any new vocabulary.

 Home-School Connection

Help your child understand the link between certain words and various holidays. Choose a national holiday, such as Martin Luther King Jr. Day. Work together to write a list of history words or social studies vocabulary associated with that day. Be prepared to prompt your child with words such as "freedom", "civil rights," and "leader."

SAMPLE QUESTION

What is the meaning of the word "holiday"? Use details from the text to support your answer.

SAMPLE STUDENT ANSWER

A holiday is a "special day" that honors a person, a group of people, or an event.

CLUE 1: This phrase answers the question by defining the word "holiday."

CLUE 2: This statement provides more details about the meaning of the word "holiday."

Now refer to the text to answer the following questions.

1. In paragraph 2, what does the word "national" mean? Use details from the passage to support your answer.

_____

_____

_____

2. In paragraph 1, what is the meaning of the word "proposed"?

   A. honored

   B. started

   C. suggested

   D. withdrew

3. This has question two parts.

First answer Part A. Then answer Part B.

Part A

What does the word "marched" mean as it is used in paragraph 3?

   A. voted for a specific government

   B. ate with friends

   C. walked with a group of people

   D. played music loudly

Part B

Which of the following details **best** supports your answer to Part A?

   E. "City Hall"

   F. "with a picnic"

   G. "popular place"

   H. "ten thousand workers"

4. What is the meaning of the word "union" as it is used in paragraph 1?

   A. a group of workers

   B. a type of job

   C. a season

   D. a family

5. What is the meaning of the word "legislation" as it is used in paragraph 4? Choose **two** answers.

   A. a fee

   B. a law

   C. a rule

   D. a date

   E. a party

6. Why is Labor Day an important holiday in the United States? Use details from the text to support your response.

   _____

   _____

   _____

0	1–2	3–4	5–6	7–8	9–10
very happy, no pain	hurts just a little bit	hurts a little more	hurts even more	hurts a whole lot	hurts as much as possible

What a Pain!

1 *Ouch!* That pan is hot! *Ow!* That bruise really hurts! *Oof!* My tummy aches.

2 No one wants to feel these sensations. But you need them. Pain is a very important reaction of your body.

3 Pain is a message from your body to your brain. It says, "Take your hand off that hot pan so you don't get burned." It warns, "Watch how you play so you don't get injured. No one wants to sit out the rest of soccer season!" It also shouts, "Pay attention to me! You might need a doctor. You don't want this illness to get worse."

4 Nerves are the body's pain messengers. Nerve fibers run throughout the entire body. They pick up messages from your skin and other organs. They carry these messages into your spinal cord and then up into the brain.

5 Each person experiences pain differently. Some people seem to have a very high tolerance for pain. They may be able to perform extreme sports and activities that other people can't. Very small numbers of people are born without being able to feel pain at all. They must be extremely careful so that they don't really hurt themselves.

6 Doctors and nurses use a pain scale to help determine how to treat a patient's pain. The pain scale runs from 1 to 10. A patient who says "My pain is a 2" probably can ride out the feeling without much help. But a patient who says "My pain is a 9" might need some pain-relieving medicine.

7 Pain is definitely a pain, but it's important all the same.

Name_____ Date_____

REVIEW THE SKILL

Science texts often include unusual words. To figure out the meaning of these words, you can use context clues, word parts (root words, prefixes, suffixes), and a dictionary.

Home-School Connections

Practice determining the meaning of scientific words and phrases with your child. Find short video clips of scientific experiments online (search for activities like "homemade volcano" or "do-it-yourself slime"). Pause the video when you hear an unfamiliar word or phrase. Then ask your child for clues that help determine the meaning.

SAMPLE QUESTION

What is the meaning of the word "aches" in paragraph 1? Use details from the text in your answer.

SAMPLE STUDENT ANSWER

Based on the title "What a Pain!" I can infer that an "ache" is a type of pain. "Ouch," "ow," and "oof" are all sounds made when someone is in pain. "Hurts" is another word that describes pain.

CLUE 1: The title of the article tells that the subject of the text is pain.

CLUE 2: Clues from the rest of the text help readers understand the meaning of the word "ache."

Now refer to "What a Pain!" to answer the following questions.

1. Define "sensations." Use details from the text to support your answer.

_____

_____

_____

2. What does the use of the word "shouts" in paragraph 3 suggest? Choose **two** answers.

   A. pain that is very strong or intense

   B. pain that is caused by loud noise

   C. pain that is difficult to ignore

   D. pain that speaks out loud

   E. pain that is mild

3. Reread this passage from the text.

   > "Nerves are the body's pain messengers. Nerve fibers run throughout the entire body. They pick up messages from your skin and other organs. They carry these messages into your spinal cord and then up into the brain."

   Which words or phrases from the text describe what a "messenger" does? Pick **two** choices.

   A. "pick up"

   B. "carry"

   C. "play"

   D. "rest"

   E. "skin"

4. What does the author mean by "Pain is definitely a pain, but it's important all the same"? Use details from the text to support your answer.

   _____

   _____

   _____

5. Look at the cause-and-effect box.

Cause	Effect
Some people are born with a high tolerance for pain.	

Which detail from the passage goes in the "effect" box?

A. "They may be able to perform extreme sports and activities that other people can't."

B. "They must be extremely careful so that they don't really hurt themselves."

C. "No one wants to have to sit out the rest of soccer season!"

D. "Each person experiences pain differently."

6. This question has two parts.

First answer Part A. Then answer Part B.

Part A

What is the meaning of "scale" as it is used in paragraph 6?

A. a weighing machine

B. a measure

C. a fish part

D. a notice

Part B

Which of the following **best** supports your answer in Part A?

E. Patients indicate different levels of pain, from 1 to 10.

F. Doctors need to know how to treat pain.

G. Some people can't feel pain at all.

H. Pain is important.

A Time to Sleep

Winter

1 Throughout cold, freezing winters, many animals seem to disappear. The bats you may have seen in the summer night sky are not there in the winter. The turtle you saw in the stream isn't there when the stream gets too cold. Where did they go? Most likely, they are curled up in their dens sleeping. These animals will sleep for the whole winter.

What Is Hibernation?

2 Some animals go into a very deep sleep called hibernation.[1] Their breathing slows. Their heart rate slows, too. This is a state of deep inactivity.[2] They will either not wake up at all or maybe wake up a couple of times during the entire winter. Animals tend to hibernate in winter because this is when food is the most scarce. Once the spring brings warm weather, they'll wake up.

Getting Ready

3 In order to spend the winter months sleeping, animals need to prepare. Throughout the summer and autumn, these animals will eat a lot. They build up body fat. This fat will be broken down by their bodies while they hibernate. Their bodies will use this fat as a source of energy while they sleep. In autumn months, they will eat a lot more than usual and fatten up quite a bit.

Who Hibernates?

4 Wood frogs, prairie dogs, and bats all hibernate. Bears are known to hibernate. Some rodents,[3] like certain squirrels and hedgehogs, also hibernate.

1. hibernation: state of sleeping through the winter without waking
2. inactivity: state of not moving
3. rodents: certain small types of animals

REVIEW THE SKILL

When we read a text, we aren't just relying on words for understanding. We also use text features, such as titles, headings, sidebars, glossaries, and bolded words.

SAMPLE QUESTION

What words are in bold in the text? Why are these words in bold? Use details from the text to support your answer.

SAMPLE STUDENT ANSWER

There are several words in bold in the text, such as "Winter," "What Is Hibernation?" "Getting Ready," and "Who Hibernates?" These words are in bold because they are headers that show there will be new information.

DETAIL 1: This statement identifies bolded words in the text.

DETAIL 2: This statement explains why words in are bold.

Now refer to "A Time to Sleep" to answer the questions.

1. Look at the footnotes. What does the word "inactivity" mean? Use details from the text to support your answer.

_____

_____

_____

2. If you wanted to learn more about the main idea of the text, which key word from the text would you enter in an Internet search engine?

   A. "animals"

   B. "hibernation"

   C. "sleeping"

   D. "winter"

3. What is the meaning of the word "scarce" in paragraph 2?

   A. dry

   B. plentiful

   C. frightening

   D. in short supply

4. Which parts of the passage give details about the specific animals that hibernate? Choose **two.**

   A. Winter

   B. Getting Ready

   C. Who Hibernates?

   D. What Is Hibernation?

Conquer New Standards: Informational Text • Grade 3 • © Newmark Learning, LLC

5. This question has two parts.

First answer Part A. Then answer Part B.

Part A

If you wanted to know more about the word "rodents," where would you look in the passage?

A. the title

B. the footnotes

C. the section titled "Winter"

D. the section titled "What Is Hibernation?"

Part B

Which of the following explanations **best** supports your answer to Part A?

E. The section titled "What Is Hibernation?" contains the most important information in the passage.

F. The section titled "Winter" describes how rodents act in winter.

G. The section titled "Winter" is the first section in the text.

H. The footnotes give a definition for the word "rodents."

6. Imagine that you were going to add a separate section to the text about how bears hibernate. Write a heading for that section. Explain why you chose that particular heading.

_____

_____

_____

Johann Gutenberg: The World's Best Type of Inventor

The story of how one man's idea shaped our lives forever

1   There is an abundance of printed information in the world. There are millions of books, magazines, and newspapers. Whom can we thank for this? The genius Johann Gutenberg, creator of history's greatest invention, the printing press.

2   Sure, there are many wonderful innovations that have made life better for humans: the car or telephone. But the printing press is the most impressive of all.

3   Before the invention of the printing press, few books were published. They had to be written by hand one painstaking letter at a time. Most people could not afford them. As a result, only certain scholars and monks could read and write.

4   In 1440, this mastermind made movable type. Before that, printers had to carve an entire page of text into a block of wood. Thanks to movable type, printers could move metal letters around the page and even reuse them.

5   By 1500, printing shops had opened in the world's major cities. Newspapers began to be printed too. Nicholas Copernicus published his controversial book *On the Revolutions of Heavenly Spheres*. This book challenged the popular idea that the sun revolved around Earth.

6   Books spread knowledge across the world. As books became more available, more people learned to read. Different types of books emerged. Almanacs, travel books, collections of poetry, novels, and printed music were in demand.

7   Movable type has given people all over the world access to information and ideas. Sharing information helps people learn, and learning is the key to creating new inventions. That's why inventors past, present, and future can thank Johann Gutenberg for the gift of print.

REVIEW THE SKILL

An author's point of view is the opinion or standpoint that the author holds. Look at the ideas emphasized in the text and words that show opinion.

Home-School Connections

Help your child understand author's point of view. Discuss a controversial issue, such as the distribution of chores or permitted screen time. Ask your child to write a paragraph describing his or her opinion as you write your own opinion. Compare your paragraphs. Highlight or underline words that describe thoughts and feelings.

SAMPLE QUESTION

What do the title and subtitle tell you about the author's point of view? Use details from the text to support your answer.

SAMPLE STUDENT ANSWER

The headline and subhead of the article show the idea that the author thinks Johann Gutenberg is the greatest inventor of all time. The title includes the word "best," and the subheading says Gutenberg "shaped our lives forever."

CLUE 1: This word tells us how the author feels about Gutenberg.

CLUE 2: This detail tells us that the author thinks Gutenberg's work is important.

Now refer to the text to answer the following questions.

1. According to the author, how did Johann Gutenberg change the world? Use details from the text to support your answer.

_____

_____

_____

2. Which of the following details **best** reveals the author's point of view on Johann Gutenberg?

   A. "there are many wonderful innovations that have made life better for humans: the car or telephone"

   B. "Nicholas Copernicus published his controversial book *On the Revolutions of Heavenly Spheres.*"

   C. "printers had to carve an entire page of text into a block of wood"

   D. "In 1440, this mastermind made movable type."

3. Which ideas from the text **best** support the claim that there were fewer books available to people before the printing press came along? Choose **two.**

   A. Only scholars and monks knew how to read books.

   B. Printers were very skilled at making books.

   C. Books spread knowledge across the world.

   D. Books were only owned by the very rich.

   E. There are many important inventions.

4. What is the meaning of the word "movable" in paragraph 4?

   A. easily read

   B. able to print

   C. in one place

   D. able to be moved

5. This has question two parts.

First answer Part A. Then answer Part B.

Part A

Look at the cause-and-effect box.

Cause	Effect
	Books spread knowledge across the world.

Which detail from the passage goes in the "cause" box?

A. More people learned to read.

B. People carved each page of a book into wood.

C. Johann Gutenberg invented the printing press.

D. The inventor of the phone read a book by Johann Gutenberg.

Part B

What explanation **best** supports your answer to Part A?

E. The printing press made it easier to print more books for more people.

F. More people became inventors because there were more books to read.

G. When people used a printing press, they learned how to read.

H. Books printed with wood were highly valued worldwide.

6. According to the author, how does Gutenberg's invention continue to improve people's lives? Use details from the text to support your answer.

_____

_____

_____

A Peek at Fiji

1   Welcome to Fiji! Use this handy guide as you island-hop around this beautiful and tropical country.

2   Fiji is located in the heart of the South Pacific Ocean. It is part of Oceania, the world's smallest continent. Oceania also includes Australia and New Zealand.

3   Fiji is an archipelago, or chain of small islands. More than 332 islands were created from volcanoes 150 million years ago.

4   Fiji's main island is Viti Levu. Vanua Levu is its second largest island. About 70 percent of Fijians live on these islands. Only 100 of Fiji's islands are inhabited by people. The rest of the islands are nature reserves.

5   The Great Sea Reef is off the shores of Vanua Levu. It is the world's third largest reef system. Fish, dolphins, and turtles live here. Some 70,000 Fijian natives depend on the reef for food. But overfishing caused a decline in the fish population. The government banned fishing in certain areas.

6   The far-flung northwestern island of Rotuma is home to a small ethnic group. The Rotuman culture is like that of its Tongan neighbors. Rotuma works hard to resist outside influences. That's why tourism on Rotuma is discouraged.

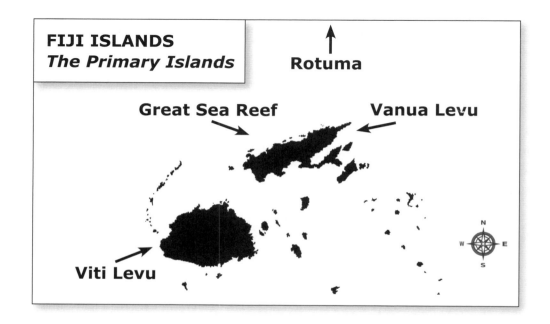

FIJI ISLANDS
The Primary Islands
Rotuma
Great Sea Reef   Vanua Levu
Viti Levu

REVIEW THE SKILL

To understand a text, look at the illustrations that go with it. The illustrations will help you understand what you read in the text.

SAMPLE QUESTION

Where is Vanua Levu located? Use details from the text and map to support your answer.

SAMPLE STUDENT ANSWER

Vanua Levu is part of the Fiji islands. It is to the northeast of Viti Levu. It is part of the continent of Oceania. Its neighbors are Australia and New Zealand.

DETAIL 1: This detail shows where Vanua Levu is on the map.

DETAIL 2: These details about Vanua Levu are from the text.

Now refer to "A Peek at Fiji" to answer the following questions.

1. Where is Viti Levu located? Use details from the text and map to support your answer.

_____

_____

_____

2. Where is the Great Sea Reef?

    A. It is off the shores of New Zealand.

    B. It is off the shores of Vanua Levu.

    C. It is off the shores of Viti Levu.

    D. It is off the shores of Rotuma.

3. This has question two parts.

    First answer Part A. Then answer Part B.

Part A

    Which of the following statements is **most likely** true?

    A. Fiji contains only two islands (Vanua Levu and Viti Levu).

    B. Rotuma is the largest island in the South Pacific Ocean.

    C. Fiji is mostly made up of hundreds of small islands.

    D. All of the Fiji islands contain active volcanoes.

Part B

    Which of the following explanations **best** supports your answer to Part A?

    E. Vanua Levu and Viti Levu are labeled on the map.

    F. The map shows many tiny islands that are part of Fiji.

    G. The map does not actually show the island of Rotuma.

    H. The passage says that the Fiji islands were formed millions of years ago.

4. If a person wanted to travel from Vanua Levu to Viti Levu, in which direction should the person travel?

    A. northwest

    B. southwest

    C. northeast

    D. southeast

5. Reread this excerpt from paragraph 5.

> "But overfishing caused a decline in the fish population. The government banned fishing in certain areas."

Which of the following phrases **best** describe the meaning of "banned"? Choose **two.**

    A. had a record-breaking success

    B. made illegal everywhere

    C. prevented further destruction

    D. recovered from a setback

    E. grew worse over time

    F. officially stopped an activity

6. Why might it be easy for Rotuma to preserve its culture and keep away outsiders? Use details from the text and the map to support your answer.

_____

_____

_____

A Walk like No Other

1   Historic steps were taken on July 20, 1969. American astronauts Neil Armstrong and Edwin "Buzz" Aldrin became the first two people to walk on the moon. Armstrong snapped this photograph of his colleague.

2   Their vehicle touched down on the region known as the Sea of Tranquility. Early astronomers who studied the moon made a mistake by calling this spot a "sea." There is no water here, or anywhere on the moon. Armstrong and Aldrin walked on a wide, rocky plain. Black sky loomed in every direction. There was no sign of life, no humans, animals, or plants. And it was colder than any place on Earth.

3   Armstrong took the first step onto the moon's surface. He famously remarked, "That's one small step for man, one giant leap for mankind." Aldrin followed him. He later described the moon as "a magnificent desolation."

4   Aldrin's words spoke to the importance of where they stood. The moon was more than a desolate or bleak landscape. It was the place that humans had imagined for centuries. And the astronauts' mission was the result of years of hard work. Humans went from dreaming about the moon to developing the technology to get there. Indeed, this was a magnificent moment. The photo Armstrong took of Aldrin was more than a vacation souvenir. It was proof of how far humans can go.

REVIEW THE SKILL

Illustrations and texts work together. Often, illustrations provide supporting details to the main ideas and details in a text.

 Home-School Connection

Help your child understand the saying "A picture is worth a thousand words." Discuss how pictures can help us understand important ideas. Ask your child to come up with questions about a text. Then go to a library together or go online and search for illustrations that can help your child answer these questions.

SAMPLE QUESTION

Where was the photograph taken? Use specific details from the text and the photograph to support your answer.

SAMPLE STUDENT ANSWER

This photo was taken on the moon in the area known as the "Sea of Tranquility." The passage states that Neil Armstrong and Buzz Aldrin were the first two people to walk on the moon, where "Armstrong snapped this photo of his colleague."

DETAIL 1: This detail tells us the specific area of the moon where the photo was taken.

DETAIL 2: These details tell us that this picture was taken during the first walk on the moon.

Now refer to "A Walk like No Other" to answer the following questions.

1. How do the photograph and the illustration help you understand the details in the text? Use details from all three to support your answer.

_____

_____

_____

2. Look at the photograph. Who took this photograph?

    A. Edwin Aldrin

    B. Neil Armstrong

    C. Lance Armstrong

    D. a Russian astronaut

3. Which of the following statements is true?

    A. Russia was the first nation to land on the moon.

    B. The astronauts put a flag on the moon.

    C. The astronauts were very tired.

    D. The moon was covered in water.

4. Which details from the text does the photograph support?
Choose **two.**

    A. "Black sky loomed in every direction."

    B. "And it was colder than any place on Earth."

    C. "Early astronomers who studied the moon made a mistake"

    D. "There was no sign of life, no humans, animals, or plants."

    E. "the astronauts' mission was the result of years of hard work"

5. This has question two parts.

First answer Part A. Then answer Part B.

Part A

What is the meaning of the word "landscape"?

   A. the view from a space shuttle

   B. the way a place or area looks

   C. a large image of the sky

   D. a piece of land

Part B

Which detail from the passage **best** describes the moon's landscape?

   E. "their vehicle touched down"

   F. "one giant leap for mankind"

   G. "wide, rocky plain"

   H. "the Sea of Tranquility"

6. How are the photograph and illustration similar and different? Use details from the text, the photograph, and the illustration to support your answer.

_____

_____

_____

How to Wrap a Perfect Burrito

Ingredients you'll need:

1   • A large flour tortilla

2   • A filling. Choose from scrambled eggs, tofu, beans, rice, grilled meat, or vegetables.

3   • A topping. Consider chopped avocado, fresh cilantro, hot sauce, or salsa.

Directions:

4   **Step 1.** Heat a tortilla in the microwave for five seconds. Or get an adult's help to warm it in a skillet.

5   **Step 2.** Place the tortilla on a plate. Imagine there is a horizontal line across the center of the tortilla. Spoon filling on the bottom half of the tortilla. Don't overfill. Leave space around it. If you don't, your tortilla might rip.

6   **Step 3.** Add your toppings. Be careful to sprinkle them sparingly. You don't want your burrito to get soggy.

7   **Step 4.** Fold side 1 toward the imaginary center vertical line. Fold side 2 toward the imaginary vertical line.

8   **Step 5.** Bring up the bottom of the tortilla. Tuck it around the filling.

9   **Step 6.** Roll the burrito snugly one time to hold in the filling. Don't roll it too tight! Roll it again. Roll it for the last time. You've made a perfect burrito!

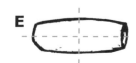

REVIEW THE SKILL

As you read the passage, think about what the pictures show. Then think about how the words explain the concepts in the pictures.

Home-School Connection

Help your child understand the connections between illustrations and text. Have your child first look at the illustrations on the previous page without reading the words. Ask your child to describe what's happening in the pictures. After reading the passage, discuss how the illustrations do or do not match the text.

SAMPLE QUESTION

What will you need to make the perfect burrito? Use details from the text and illustration to support your answer.

SAMPLE STUDENT ANSWER

Illustration A shows that I will need a large, circular object and something called "filling." The section "Ingredients you'll need" helps me understand that I need a large flour tortilla, a filling, and a topping.

CLUE 1: The diagram shows the items needed in general.

CLUE 2: The text tells the items needed specifically.

Now refer to "How to Wrap a Perfect Burrito" to answer the following questions.

1. Explain where the fillings and toppings belong on the tortilla. Use details from the text and illustrations to support your answer.

_____

_____

_____

2. Why don't the fillings go to the edges of the tortilla?
   Pick **two** reasons.

   A. so the tortilla doesn't rip

   B. so the tortilla stays warm

   C. so the counter stays clean

   D. so the burrito tastes better

   E. so the burrito doesn't get overfilled

3. What is the meaning of "snugly" as it is used in paragraph 9?

   A. in a cozy way

   B. in a loose way

   C. in a tight way

   D. in a sloppy way

4. Based on the illustrations, in which direction should the tortilla be rolled after folding in the sides?

   A. starting from the left and rolling to the right

   B. starting from the top and rolling to the bottom

   C. starting from the right and rolling to the left

   D. starting from the bottom and rolling to the top

5. This has question two parts.

First answer Part A. Then answer Part B.

Part A

How should sides 1 and 2 of the tortilla be folded?

- **A.** They should be folded upward toward the imaginary horizontal line.
- **B.** They should be folded downward toward the imaginary horizontal line.
- **C.** They should be folded sideways toward the imaginary vertical line.
- **D.** They should be folded sideways toward the imaginary horizontal line.

Part B

Which detail **best** supports your answer to Part A?

- **E.** Step 1
- **F.** Step 6
- **G.** Illustration D
- **H.** Illustration C

6. In your own words, explain steps 5 and 6 of the burrito-making process. Use details from the text and illustrations in your answer.

_____

_____

_____

Moth or Butterfly?

1   Butterflies and moths add beauty and magic to the world around us. They flutter through our gardens. They glide peacefully through the air. At first glance, the two species may seem very similar. We must look closer to understand the differences between them.

2   Most butterflies are very bright and colorful. In contrast, moths are usually drab. However, there are exceptions to this rule. The wings of a cecropia moth have splashes of red. The cabbage white butterfly is bland, pale yellow-white. Both species are covered with scales.

3   There is one easy way to tell how moths and butterflies differ. Look at the antennae. A butterfly's antenna is like a club. It is a long shaft with a bulb at the end. The antenna of a moth is feathery, or edged like a saw.

4   Butterflies and moths hold their wings differently. Moths usually hold their wings spread out flat or folded together over their backs, hiding their abdomen. Butterflies tend to fold their wings up straight over their backs vertically.

5   Butterflies mostly fly in the daytime and rest at night. Most moths are nocturnal and do the opposite.

6   Moths and butterflies both make a similar transition from larva to pupa and then adult. The young caterpillars spin protective cases around themselves as they enter the pupa stage. Moth caterpillars spin a cocoon out of silk. A butterfly caterpillar makes a chrysalis. A chrysalis is similar to a cocoon, but it is hard and smooth. It has no silk covering.

7   Butterflies and moths have some similarities, but many differences, too. Getting to know them better is a good way to appreciate the wonder of them both.

Conquer New Standards: Informational Text • Grade 3 • © Newmark Learning, LLC

Name_____ Date_____

Home-School Connection

Help your child understand how two different things can share similarities. Use a dandelion as an example. Discuss how a dandelion compares to another flowering plant, like a daisy or a rose. Explain how it shares many of the same qualities of a flower but is actually considered a weed.

SAMPLE QUESTION

What are the similarities between moths and butterflies? Use details from paragraph 1 in your answer.

SAMPLE STUDENT ANSWER

Butterflies and moths add beauty to the world. They both "flutter through our gardens" and "glide peacefully through the air."

DETAIL 1: This detail tells something that moths and butterflies both do.

DETAIL 2: These details describe something else moths and butterflies have in common.

Now refer to "Moth or Butterfly?" to answer the questions.

1. How are the colors of most moths different from those of butterflies? Use details from the text to support your answer.

_____

_____

_____

2. How is the cecropia moth different from other moths?

  A. It is diurnal, unlike other moths.

  B. It is duller in color than other moths.

  C. It is brighter in color than other moths.

  D. It does not have scales, unlike other moths.

3. Which of the following phrases **best** describe a moth that is "nocturnal"? Pick **two** choices.

  A. awake at night

  B. asleep at night

  C. awake during the day

  D. asleep during the day

  E. awake during the day and night

4. How is the way a moth holds its wings **different** from the way a butterfly holds its wings?

  A. Moths fold their wings straight up over their backs, whereas butterflies fold their wings over their abdomens.

  B. Moths fold their wings over their abdomens, whereas butterflies fold their wings straight over their backs.

  C. Moths fold their wings over their abdomens, whereas butterflies fold their wings so they are spread out.

  D. Moths fold their wings so they are spread out, whereas butterflies fold their wings over their abdomens.

5. This has question two parts.

First answer Part A. Then answer Part B.

Part A

Imagine a butterfly is in front of you. What is one way to know that it is **not** a moth?

  A. It has club-shaped antennae.

  B. It is dull in color.

  C. It has scales.

  D. It is flying.

Part B

Which answer choice **best** supports your answer in Part A?

  E. "Butterflies mostly fly in the daytime and rest at night."

  F. "Look at the antennae."

  G. "The antenna of a moth is feathery, or edged like a saw."

  H. "It is a long shaft with a bulb at the end."

6. Explain the differences and similarities in how moths and butterflies transition from caterpillar to adult. Use details from the text to support your answer.

_____

_____

_____

Why Flamingos Are Pink

1   A flamingo's color comes from a surprising source. For them, the old saying is true: you are what you eat.

2   The pink flamingo is born with gray feathers. The rosy color comes from the flamingo's main food source: the brine shrimp. These tiny shrimp feed on microscopic algae. These algae contain carotenoids. Carotenoids produce the colors of a plant. The orange in carrots is an example of a carotenoid. If a flamingo stopped eating brine shrimp, its feathers would eventually turn back to gray.

3   Flamingos are not the only birds to absorb color from their food. Northern cardinals and goldfinches do too. These birds eat berries from trees. The seeds from these berries contain carotenoids. Like the flamingo, the cardinal's red feathers and the goldfinch's bright yellow feathers would fade without plant pigments.

4   A canary's yellow color does not depend on its diet. But it may take on a different hue if the bird is fed paprika or red pepper. These spices contain red carotenoids. Eating them could result in the canary's feathers turning deep orange.

What About Humans?

5   If a person is looking a little orange-y, food may be the reason. Eating large amounts of carrots and pumpkin can add a yellow-orange tint to the skin. These brightly colored vegetables contain beta-carotene. This carotenoid is rich in vitamin A. It is mostly harmless to the human body even if consumed in large amounts. And as with our feathered friends, this hue will fade once carotenoids are eliminated.

REVIEW THE SKILL

An effect is something that happens. A cause is why it happens. In a cause-and-effect text, the author describes the relationship between the cause and the effect.

Home-School Connection

Help your child understand cause-and-effect relationships within a text. Read a favorite story together. Pause at key moments to ask "Why did that happen?" Explain how the answer to the question is the cause of a situation. Also ask, "What happened as a result?" Explain that this is a result.

SAMPLE QUESTION

What cause-and-effect relationship is suggested by the title? Use details to support your answer.

SAMPLE STUDENT ANSWER

The title is "Why Flamingos Are Pink." The word "why" indicates a reason, or cause, that something happened. In this case, we will learn about the "why," or cause, of the flamingos' coloring. The flamingos' color is the effect.

DETAIL 1: "Why" is a word that signals the cause of something.

DETAIL 2: "Flamingos are pink" is the effect.

Now refer to the text to answer the following questions.

1. How do a flamingo's feathers get their pink color? Use details from the text to support your answer.

_____

_____

_____

Name_____ Date_____

2. Where do brine shrimp get carotenoids?

   A. algae

   B. carrots

   C. seeds

   D. water

3. What would happen to a cardinal if it stopped eating berries from trees?

   A. It would turn pink.

   B. It would absorb color from food.

   C. Its feathers would lose their color.

   D. It would have to eat more red peppers.

4. Look at the cause-and-effect box.

Cause	Effect
	A person's skin looks orange.

Which sentences or phrases go in the "cause" box?
Choose **two.**

   A. The person has been eating brine shrimp.

   B. The person has been eating red pepper.

   C. The person has been eating pumpkins.

   D. The person has been eating carrots.

   E. The person has been eating algae.

5. This has question two parts.

First answer Part A. Then answer Part B.

Part A

What is the meaning of the word "tint" as it is used in paragraph 5?

A. color

B. food

C. light

D. shadow

Part B

Which sentence from the passage contains a **synonym** for "tint"?

E. "this hue will fade once carotenoids are eliminated"

F. "It is mostly harmless to the human body"

G. "This carotenoid is rich in vitamin A."

H. "food may be the reason"

6. Describe the effect of eating red pepper on a canary. Use details from the text to support your answer.

_____

_____

_____

Inside a Native American Naming Ceremony

1 Some Native American Indians have more than one name. They have the name they are given at birth. But they may also want a new name to show how they have changed throughout life.

2 Certain actions must be completed before the new name is official. First, he or she will ask a tribe elder for a new name. Then the person gives the elder a gift of herbs. This is known as *kicnic-kicnic.* The herbs are passed from the person's left hand to the elder's left hand. This symbolizes the idea of passing something from one heart to another.

3 After the elder gives permission, preparations begin for a special ceremony. In the meantime, the elder thinks about the new name a lot. The elder may choose this name while in a dream or vision state.

4 Next is the ceremony. The person getting the new name will stand in the middle of a prayer circle. A fire is lit. The elder chooses four guides to act as witnesses. At the end of the ceremony, the elder announces the new name. But that doesn't mean the recipient can use it immediately. Instead, the elder will decide when the person is ready to be called by the new name. That can take weeks, or even years.

5 The last step of the name-changing process is for the recipient to thank everyone who attended. He or she will host a meal for them. This celebration always features music and song.

REVIEW THE SKILL

To understand the sequence of a text, review its major points and events. Look for connecting words, such as "first," "then," "next," and "in the end."

Home-School Connection

Help your child understand sequencing. Review the steps of a recipe or craft together. Then have your child write down the steps needed to prepare a favorite meal. Review your child's list, and work together to add sequencing words such as "first," "next," and "last."

SAMPLE QUESTION

Describe the first step that a Native American person takes in order to get a new name. Use details from the text to support your answer.

SAMPLE STUDENT ANSWER

The person who wants a new name must ask a tribe elder for a new name. I know this is the first step because the second sentence of the second paragraph begins with the word "First," then follows with "he or she will ask a tribe elder for a new name."

CLUE 1: This word is a clue as to the order of events.

CLUE 2: This detail describes what happens during the first step.

Now refer to the text to answer the following questions.

1. Describe what happens after the person asks an elder for a new name. Use details from the text to support your answer.

_____

_____

_____

2. What happens after the elder gives permission for a new name?

   A. There is dancing.

   B. Herbs are given.

   C. The new name is announced.

   D. A special ceremony is planned.

3. What happens after the person stands in the prayer circle? Pick **two** choices.

   A. A fire is lit.

   B. The elder reads a book.

   C. The elder will get a gift.

   D. The elder chooses four guides.

   E. The elder will go into a dream or vision state.

4. Events from "Inside a Native American Naming Ceremony" are listed below. Put the order of the events of the naming ceremony in the correct sequence.

   A. A fire is lit.

   B. The elder chooses four witnesses.

   C. A person asks an elder for a new name.

   D. The person stands in the middle of a prayer circle.

   E. The elder decides when the new name can be used.

1. ____ 2. ____ 3. ____ 4. ____ 5. ____

5. This has question two parts.

First answer Part A. Then answer Part B.

Part A

What does the word "immediately" mean as it is used in paragraph 4?

A. in a while

B. sometime today

C. without any delay

D. in an uncertain amount of time

Part B

Which sentence from the text **best** supports your answer in Part A?

E. "In the meantime, the elder thinks about the new name a lot."

F. "At the end of the ceremony, the elder announces the new name."

G. "Certain actions must be completed before the new name is official."

H. "Instead, the elder will decide when the person is ready to be called by the new name."

6. What are the three major steps taken to get a new name? Use details from the text to support your answer.

_____

_____

_____

Misty Copeland Changes the Face of Ballet

1   Misty Copeland is changing the face of ballet in America. In the summer of 2015, Misty became the first African American principal dancer in the American Ballet Theatre (ABT). Founded in 1937 in New York City, ABT is one of the world's leading classical ballet companies. A principal holds the highest rank in a ballet company.

2   Misty started dancing at 13, at an age that is older than most professional ballerinas start. She had a tough life at home. The family struggled. They had even lived in a motel room for a while. Misty and her siblings had to sleep on the floor. Her mother didn't have a car. Misty couldn't get to ballet lessons. Thankfully, she met a ballet teacher who arranged for her to continue practicing.

3   Within three months, Misty was wearing pointe shoes. This usually takes other dancers years to achieve. As the years went on, Misty achieved many accomplishments in the world of ballet. The news of her talent spread.

4   Still, Misty faced prejudice from people who thought that only white dancers belonged in ballet. However, many more people became fans. Now Misty is trying to help other minority dancers. She is involved with Project Plié. This organization is working to bring ballet to people of all backgrounds.

Misty Copeland Dances Into History

1   Misty Copeland is the first African American principal dancer in the history of the American Ballet Theatre (ABT). She is also the first African American to play the lead role in *Swan Lake*.

2   Copeland's breakout role at ABT was in *The Firebird* in 2012. She played the firebird itself. It was a difficult role. Pain in her left shin nagged her during and after rehearsals. She didn't want to be replaced, so she continued dancing. She didn't tell anyone how much she was hurting.

3   Copeland gave a stunning performance on opening night. Critics were dazzled. Only after the show did she admit to how much pain she was in. She finally went to the doctor and learned that she had six near-breaks in her lower leg bone. Her leg could have completely broken anytime during rehearsals and performance.

4   The injury could be repaired only through surgery. Copeland had a metal plate put into her shin. Bone marrow was taken from her hip and put into the breaks in her bone. She spent weeks learning how to walk again.

5   It was an injury that would have ended the career of many dancers. But Copeland was performing just eight months later. In 2014, she starred in a popular commercial for athletic wear, which has been viewed more than eight million times on YouTube. She also published two books. *Life in Motion* is an autobiography. *Firebird* is a book for kids.

REVIEW THE SKILL

To integrate information from two texts, we identify key details in each text. Then we compare those details to see which are the same and which are different.

Home-School Connection

Help your child compare two texts. Select two local news articles about the same topic. Together, take notes about the important points in each article. Ask your child to identify similarities and differences between the two articles. Then ask your child to draw an inference based on the details in both articles.

SAMPLE QUESTION

How are the first paragraphs of each passage similar? How are they different? Use details from the texts to support your answer.

SAMPLE STUDENT ANSWER

Each text begins by saying that Misty Copeland is the first African American principal dancer at the American Ballet Theatre. The first text then describes the American Ballet Theatre. The second text talks about Copeland in "Swan Lake."

DETAIL 1: This point is shared by the two passages.

DETAIL 2: These are points that the two passages do not have in common.

Now refer to both texts to answer the following questions.

1. Discuss the different ways each passage refers to Misty Copeland, and then describe how this affects the tone of the passage. Use examples from each text to support your answer.

_____

_____

_____

2. Which of the passages describes incidents from Misty Copeland's childhood?

    A. "Misty Copeland Changes the Face of Ballet"

    B. Neither of the texts discusses her childhood.

    C. Both of the texts discuss her childhood.

    D. "Misty Copeland Dances Into History"

3. This has question two parts.

First answer Part A. Then answer Part B.

Part A

What is the meaning of the word "struggled" as it is used in paragraph 2 of "Misty Copeland Changes the Face of Ballet"?

    A. worked hard

    B. helped each other

    C. had a difficult time

    D. didn't have any money

Part B

Which statement **best** supports your answer in Part A?

    E. The family clearly cared for each other because they shared the motel room.

    F. The family must have worked a lot in order to pay for a motel room.

    G. The family did not have a home of their own, a car, or an easy life.

    H. Misty began wearing pointe shoes within a few months.

4. Which of the passages **best** shows Copeland's dedication to ballet? Use details from the text to support your answer.

_____

_____

_____

5. Which sentence from "Misty Copeland Dances Into History" **best** shows the author's point of view?

   A. "It was a difficult role."

   B. "The injury could be repaired only through surgery."

   C. "Copeland gave a stunning performance on opening night."

   D. "Bone marrow was taken from her hip and put into the breaks in her bone."

6. Events from both passages are listed below. Put the events in the right order on the time line.

   A. Copeland stars in a commercial.

   B. Copeland dances the role of the firebird.

   C. Copeland and her family live in a motel.

   D. Copeland is named a principal dancer at ABT.

   E. Copeland undergoes surgery for a nearly-broken leg.

   1. ____ 2. ____ 3. ____ 4. ____ 5. ____

7. This question has two parts.
First, answer Part A. Then, answer Part B.

Part A

What challenge did Misty still face even after years of success?

A. a tough home life

B. constant injuries

C. bad press

D. racism

Part B

Which statement from "Misty Copeland Changes the Face of Ballet" best supports your answer in Part A?

E. "Misty couldn't get to ballet lessons."

F. "As the years went on, Misty achieved many accomplishments in the world of ballet."

G. "Thankfully, she met a ballet teacher who arranged for her to continue practicing."

H. "Still, Misty faced prejudice from people who thought that only white dancers belonged in ballet."

8. Which passage **best** indicates why it is so remarkable that Misty Copeland is a principal dancer at ABT? Use details from the passage to support your answer.

_____

_____

_____

Unit 1: Discussion Prompts

1. The detail that helped me understand the text the most was…

2. Using the details in the text helped because…

3. I think this skill is important because…

 AT-HOME ACTIVITIES: *Details Race*

Stand with your child against the wall on the side of a room. Take turns recalling a detail from the unit text. Each time a person correctly recalls a detail, the person can take one step forward. The person who correctly recalls the most details and gets to the other side of the room first wins!

Unit 2: Discussion Prompts

1. I am still curious about…

2. I am confused and have questions about…

3. Answering my questions with details helped me by…

 AT-HOME ACTIVITIES: *Question-and-Answer Shopping Spree*

Get sticky notes and canned food. Together with your child, brainstorm questions about the text in the unit. Write one question on each sticky note and place the note on a can of food. Tell your child he or she has one minute to try to answer as many questions on the cans as possible. Set the timer and let the shopping spree begin! Take turns until all the cans are used.

Unit 3: Discussion Prompts

1. The main idea of this paragraph was...
2. Some of the main ideas in the text are...
3. This unit skill helped me...

 AT-HOME ACTIVITIES: *Main Idea Madness!*

Pick different texts to read with your child, such as newspaper articles, recipes, and science books. For each one, practice a different technique for determining the main idea, such as looking at the title and reading the first paragraph; circling when the same words occur in each paragraph; and looking for a concluding sentence in the final paragraph.

Unit 4: Discussion Prompts

1. The text was mostly about...
2. The idea from the text I remember best is...
3. Recounting the key ideas helped me...

 AT-HOME ACTIVITIES: *Operator*

Play this game with your child and other friends or family members. Read one paragraph of the unit text to your child in another room. Return, and have your child retell one of the key ideas from the paragraph by whispering in another person's ear. This person should whisper the key idea to another person, and so on. At the end, read the paragraph aloud and discuss the key idea and if it was forgotten or changed.

Unit 5: Discussion Prompts

1. A key idea is…

2. This key idea in the text… supports the text's main topic.

3. This idea in the text… does not support the text's main topic.

 AT-HOME ACTIVITIES: *Do You Agree?*

Read an article from a newspaper that is about a topic that might appeal to your child. Together, identify the author's points and supporting reasons. Then, ask your child if he or she agrees with the author's points. Does your child feel that the author included enough reasons to support the points, or not?

Unit 6: Discussion Prompts

1. Some types of relationships are…

2. The relationship between these details… is…

3. Identifying relationships helped me…

 AT-HOME ACTIVITIES: *Understanding Relationships*

Discuss with your child the different types of relationships in a text, such as sequence, compare/contrast, cause/effect, and more. Next, ask your child to create a table. The head of the first column of the table should be "Type of Relationship." Your child can create a row for each type of relationship. Then your child can identify examples of each in a second column and cite the text the example comes from in the third column.

Unit 7: Discussion Prompts

1. Two events that are connected are...
2. Some ideas connected by cause-and-effect are...
3. Some details connected by sequence are...

 AT-HOME ACTIVITIES: *Tic-Tac-Toe*

Play tic-tac-toe with your child. Begin by drawing a tic-tac-toe board (nine squares stacked in three rows of three squares). Take turns identifying connections in the historical unit text with your child. Each time either of you correctly identifies a connection, you can take a step to play tic-tac-toe.

Unit 8: Discussion Prompts

1. Two people that are connected are...
2. These details are connected by...
3. The unit skill helped me...

 AT-HOME ACTIVITIES: *Be a Scientist*

Help your child dress up like a scientist (white shirt/lab coat, notepad, pencil) and then take a science walk around the block. Notice events and discuss how they are connected. For example, you might notice the event of a bird diving to the ground to eat seeds, and so you could say that wanting to eat seeds caused the bird to dive to the ground.

Unit 9: Discussion Prompts

1. Two steps that are connected are...

2. These ideas are connected by...

3. The unit skill helped me...

 AT-HOME ACTIVITIES: *Mixed-Up PBJs*

Discuss the steps for making a peanut butter and jelly sandwich (or other food) with your child, and write these steps down. Then make a sandwich together, but do the steps out of order. Then, make another sandwich together, skipping a step. Lastly, make a sandwich together following all the steps correctly, and compare the sandwiches with your child.

Unit 10: Discussion Prompts

1. I can use context clues to...

2. When I read and find a confusing word, I can...

3. Figuring out the meaning of words helped me...

 AT-HOME ACTIVITIES: *Interview the Word*

Help your child write a list of words that he or she does not know. Encourage your child to look up each word in a dictionary. Then write the first word on a piece of paper, and stick this paper to your child's shirt, using tape. Tell your child to pretend to be this word, while you pretend to "interview" this word. Ask, "What do you mean?" and "When are you used?"

Unit 11: Discussion Prompts

1. Some social studies words I found were...

2. One social studies word that confused me was...

3. Figuring out the meaning of these words helped me...

 AT-HOME ACTIVITIES: *Writing My Own Notes*

Encourage your child to circle the social studies terms he or she finds confusing in the unit text. Then, ask your child to identify context clues to develop his or her own understanding of each unknown word. Lastly, ask your child to come up with a synonym or similar-meaning word and write this in the margin or near each word.

Unit 12: Discussion Prompts

1. Some science words I found were...

2. One science word that confused me was...

3. Figuring out the meaning of these words helped me...

 AT-HOME ACTIVITIES: *In the Margin*

Encourage your child to circle the science terms he or she finds confusing in the unit text. Then, ask your child to look up the definition of each word and write a brief version of the definition in the margin. If your child likes, he or she could also draw a diagram in the margin to help define the meaning of the science term.

Unit 13: Discussion Prompts

1. Some text features are…
2. Text features are helpful because…
3. When I look at text features, I…

 AT-HOME ACTIVITIES: _My Magazine_

Discuss different text features with your child, such as captions, bold print, glossaries, subheadings, indexes, icons, key words, and sidebars. Then encourage your child to write and draw his or her own magazine about a favorite topic. Help your child add all the text features to the magazine.

Unit 14: Discussion Prompts

1. The term "point of view" means…
2. The author's point of view in the unit text was…
3. I figured out the author's point of view by…

 AT-HOME ACTIVITIES: _Red Means No, Green Means I Agree_

Read magazine or newspaper articles with your child. Give your child red and green markers. Ask your child to underline sentences that show the authors' points of view. Instruct your child to use a red marker if he or she disagrees with the author's point of view and to use a green marker if he or she agrees with the author's point of view.

Unit 15: Discussion Prompts

1. The unit text used a map to...
2. The illustration helped me better understand...
3. The illustration... gave me this information...

 AT-HOME ACTIVITIES: *Map the Route*

Show your child various print or digital maps. Encourage your child to choose a map and plan a route from one point to another. As your child plots the trip, ask questions: What streets will we cross on our way? In what direction will we travel as we complete the route? How long will it take to get to the destination by car?

Unit 16: Discussion Prompts

1. One illustration I saw was...
2. The illustration helped me better understand...
3. The illustration... gave me this information...

 AT-HOME ACTIVITIES: *Mystery House*

Secretly create a mystery in your house, such as hiding your child's crayons or your child's favorite food. Leave clues, and take photos of the clues. Show your child the photos, and ask him or her to identify as much information as possible from these photos in order to solve the mystery. Then encourage your child to create a mystery and draw clues for you.

Unit 17: Discussion Prompts

1. Some information only in the text was…

2. Some information only in the illustrations was…

3. Information in both the text and illustrations was…

 AT-HOME ACTIVITIES: *Goofy Guidebook*

Work with your child to create a "Goofy Guidebook." First, determine the topic together (such as a recipe or hobby). Then, ask your child to write a series of steps, while you illustrate these steps. (Or you can write while your child illustrates.) When you are both done, staple your work together and review. What information was in the text? What information was in the illustrations? What information was in both?

Unit 18: Discussion Prompts

1. Two similar details were...
2. Two different details were...
3. Thinking about ways details were alike and different helped me...

 AT-HOME ACTIVITIES: *Hit the Buzzer*

Gather a buzzer or a bell and also a single number cube. Cover each side of the cube with tape. Write *S* on three sides and *D* on three sides. Take turns rolling the number cube. Landing *S*-side up means identifying two similar details in the unit text. Landing *D*-side up means identifying two different details. Whoever comes up with an answer first must ring the bell or hit the buzzer. If the person correctly identifies a similarity or difference, the person earns a point. Whoever gets 10 points first wins.

Unit 19: Discussion Prompts

1. A cause is something that...
2. An effect is something that...
3. I think... caused... to happen in the text.

 AT-HOME ACTIVITIES: *Cause-and-Effect Stroll*

Take a walk with your child. As you walk, your child should identify things he or she observes and state them as a possible cause, for example, "I feel the wind blowing very strong. This causes..." Then, you should identify a possible effect, for example, "the trees to shake."

Unit 20: Discussion Prompts

1. The first thing that happened in the unit text was…

2. The last thing that happened in the unit text was…

3. Thinking about sequence helped me…

 AT-HOME ACTIVITIES: *Chart the Sequence*

Encourage your child to draw a staircase on a large piece of poster paper. Your child should number the stairs on the staircase, beginning with the first step. Then your child should write a detail next to each stair in the order that it occurs in the unit text. Review your child's work and make sure he or she has correctly sequenced the details from the text in the drawing.

Unit 21: Discussion Prompts

1. The texts were alike in these ways...
2. The texts were different in these ways...
3. Based on these texts, I think...

 AT-HOME ACTIVITIES: *Author Debate*

Encourage your child to pick two texts by different authors about the same topic, or use the unit texts. Ask your child to draw a picture of each author, and write a sentence stating the author's key idea or point of view. Then, ask your child a question about the topic. Your child should hold the picture of the first author over his or her face and answer the question pretending to be that author. Next, your child should do the same with the picture of the second author. Discuss the ways in which the authors' answers were similar and different.

Answer Key

Unit 1

pages 14–17

1. Sample answer: The second paragraph tells us that "European countries were fighting in a war." The author uses the phrase "at the time" to tell us that the war was going on when Roosevelt gave his speech. The text also tells us that Great Britain was fighting against Germany.

2. Sample answer: The Four Freedoms are freedom of speech, freedom of worship, freedom from want, and freedom from fear. The first two freedoms mean that people should be able to speak their minds and worship as they want. The last two freedoms mean that everyone should have adequate food, clothing, and shelter, and they should feel safe where they live.

3. **B, F**   The Four Freedoms are freedom of speech, freedom of worship, freedom from want, and freedom from fear. Practicing medicine and making war are not mentioned.

4. **B** The text says that U.S. citizens were against fighting. Then, Roosevelt gave the speech and "the United States no longer stayed neutral."

5. **C** Paragraph 1 says that Roosevelt "wanted people everywhere in the world to enjoy" the Four Freedoms. This detail supports answer choice C.

6. **Part A**   **C**

   Part B   **H**   The word "communicate" means to express oneself. Usually this is done by talking. The clue that reveals the meaning of "communicate" is "speech," as in "Freedom of speech."

Unit 2

pages 18–21

1. Sample answer: President Roosevelt wants all people to be able to express their ideas and opinions. He thinks everyone should have medical care and unemployment insurance. He also says that people should be free from fear and want. They should have happy, healthy lives.

2. **D** In paragraph 6, Roosevelt says "our support goes to those who struggle to gain those rights."

3. **Part A**   **B**   In this paragraph, "to struggle" means to work hard or "fight for" something.

   Part B   **F, G**   The word "gain" means that you get something that you didn't have before. The word "keep" means you hang on to something. All of those words help us understand what it is like to struggle for something.

4. Sample answer: Roosevelt says that the special privilege for the few should end. Nobody should have more rights than anybody else.

     Conquer New Standards: Informational Text • Grade 3 • © Newmark Learning, LLC

Answer Key

5. A, D   The text says that Roosevelt gave the speech on January 6, 1941. The details that show how he wanted people to have these basic rights now are "in our own time" (answer choice A) and "no vision of a distant time" (answer choice D).

Unit 3

pages 22–25

1. Sample answer: Sally Ride's job was to run "the robotic arm." It was used to put satellites into space.

2. **C** The text says that after Sally went to college, she saw an ad in a newspaper. She applied for a job at NASA and was hired.

3. **Part A**   **C**   In this text, the word "honors" means "recognizes."

   Part B   **G**   When Sally Ride was inducted into the Astronaut Hall of Fame, she was recognized for all of her hard work.

4. **C** Sally Ride was the first American woman to travel to space. In addition to working for NASA, she taught science and developed a special project involving the International Space Station. That's why she was inducted into the Astronaut Hall of Fame.

5. (1) **F** She earned degrees in physics. (2) **E** She saw a NASA ad in the newspaper. (3) **B** In 1983, she was the first American woman to fly in space. (4) **C** She flew on the space shuttle again in 1984. (5) **D** She stopped working for NASA in 1987. (6) **A** She came up with a project involving a special camera.

6. Sample answer: Sally Ride got involved in science in many ways. She looked for ways to help women and girls who wanted to study science and math. She wrote science books. She came up with a project that allowed students to take pictures from space.

Unit 4

pages 26–29

1. Sample answer: The text says that rocks shaped like spoons, rats, iguanas, and elephants have been discovered on Mars.

2. **B** The detail "found only rocks" shows that scientists have not found life on Mars.

3. **C** The text contains a lot of details about how the shapes found on Mars are made from wind carving rocks, so this is a key idea.

4. Sample answer: A key idea of paragraph 6 is that wind can carve rocks into interesting shapes. Wind on Earth has carved rocks into arches and towers, and it has carved rocks on Mars, too.

5. **Part A**   **A**   The word "constant" means "nonstop."

   Part B   **H**   The detail "round-the-clock" reveals how the word "constant" describes something that is always happening, at all hours of the day, or "nonstop."

Answer Key

6. A, B   The phrase "those other shapes" and the words "rats, iguanas, and elephants" all support the idea that NASA found rocks in many different shapes on Mars.

Unit 5

pages 30–33

1. Sample answer: Chopsticks should be used with care in both China and Japan. You should not pass with them in Japan and avoid pointing with them in China.

2. **A** This detail mentions how "around the world" there are "different rules," so this detail supports the idea that people in many places follow rules when they eat.

3. **Part A   B**   In paragraph 7, the word "offensive" is used to describe an action that is "not polite."

   Part B   G   The word "rude" is a context clue that reveals that eating with your hands "in Chile" would be "offensive" or "not polite."

4. **A, B, F**   Britain has a rule that you should sip from the side of your spoon to appear fancy. Chile has a rule that you should use utensils and not your hands. Thailand has a rule that you should use a fork only to put food on a spoon.

5. **C** Answer choice C states that table manners are different in different countries, so this supports the idea that table manners are unique throughout the world.

6. Sample answer: In Egypt, I would not use salt on my food. If I did, it would insult the chef because the chef would think I didn't like the taste of the food. So I would not sprinkle extra salt on it, and this would show respect to the person who cooked the food.

Unit 6

pages 34–37

1. Sample answer: The writer Luis Coloma created the character of El Ratoncito Perez, the mouse who brings coins and presents to children in Spain and Latin America.

2. **B** The details in the passage use a compare-and-contrast structure. There are details about El Ratoncito Perez. Then there are details about La Petite Souris.

3. **C** Perez stuck his tail in the king's nose and transformed him into a mouse.

4. (1) **B** Perez visited King Bubi in the middle of the night. (2) **C** Perez put the tip of his tail in Bubi's nostril. (3) **A** Perez and Bubi traveled through the drains of the city. (4) **E** Bubi saw many poor children. (5) **D** Bubi grew up and became very generous.

5. **Part A   D**   Substituting "version" for "spin" makes the most sense in the sentence.

   Part B   E   The paragraph contains another story about the same general idea. So it tells a "version" of the tooth legend.

   Conquer New Standards: Informational Text • Grade 3 • © Newmark Learning, LLC

Answer Key

6. Sample answer: Tooth legends are told to help children be less scared of losing their teeth. The passage says these stories are to help them "feel better." Even though there are different characters in different legends, the stories still have the same purpose.

Unit 7

pages 38–41

1. Sample answer: Paragraph 3 says "Watson had been Bell's assistant." So that means Watson had worked for Bell as his assistant during the early days of telephone experimentation. They worked together on sound experiments. Together, they contributed to significant scientific achievements.

2. **A** Paragraph 5 states that "a voice signal would naturally weaken as it traveled long distances." This detail supports answer choice A.

3. **D** Bell and Watson had "spent several years" experimenting. And only because of this work was Bell able to call Watson in the next room.

4. Sample answer: The joke referred to Bell and Watson's first achievement, when Bell called Watson from only a room away. Bell said, "Mr. Watson, come here. I want you." But when Bell said it again, Watson was on the opposite coast and so he said "it will take me five days."

5. **Part A   A**   In this sentence, the word "range" is used to mean "the distance something can travel."

Part B   F   The phrase "short distances" is a context clue that reveals that the meaning of the word "range" is "distance," or "an area or place."

6. (1) **D** Alexander Graham Bell invented the telephone. (2) **E** Lee de Forest invented the Audion. (3) **C** AT&T found a device to strengthen signals. (4) **B** AT&T put Audions on telephone wires from coast to coast. (5) **A** Alexander Graham Bell called Thomas A. Watson in California.

Unit 8

pages 42–45

1. Sample answer: Because they are so small, microbes fly into the air without people knowing they are there. Humans breathe them in without knowing. Then they get sick.

2. **A** It takes millions and millions of microbes in a group to make them visible.

3. **B, E**   A colony is a "group" or a "team" of microbes that live together and form a cluster.

4. **C** These paragraphs talk about small animals like hamsters and fleas. Then they compare them to the size of microbes, which are much smaller. So these paragraphs use a compare-and-contrast structure.

5. **A** When someone sneezes, the person releases microbes into the air. Then another person inhales these germs.

Answer Key

6. Part A   **B**

    Part B   **F, I**   Microbes break down dead plants, animal waste, and garbage. This helps clean the oceans and forests.

Unit 9

pages 46–49

1. Sample answer: Tulips should be planted in a sunny spot. The text says it should be "a place that gets full or afternoon sun every day." Tulips also shouldn't be planted anywhere too wet. The text says "Tulips don't like too much moisture."

2. (1) **B** Space bulbs 4–6 inches apart on the ground. (2) **C** Dig an 8-inch-deep hole for each bulb. (3) **A** Place a bulb in each hole with the pointy end facing up. (4) **E** Cover with soil. (5) **D** Press the soil firmly.

3. **C** Bulbs only need water at first to trigger growth. Step 5 says that, after that, water will cause bulbs to "rot."

4. **D** Step 6 says to use "compost" or another organic fertilizer to feed the tulip plants.

5. **Part A**   **B**   A perennial is a plant that will return every year.

    Part B   **E, G**   "Every spring" and "year after year" are clues to the meaning of "perennial."

6. Sample answer: First, cut stems on the diagonal. Wrap upper part of stems with a funnel of newspaper. Let stand in cool water for an hour or two. Then re-cut stems.

Unit 10

pages 50–53

1. Sample answer: There had not been a garden at the White House for many years. So "broke ground" must mean that the students and the First Lady dug up the dirt to make a new garden.

2. **C** Paragraph 2 says that "the garden is planted, tended, and harvested," so the word "tended" means "taken care of."

3. **B, E** This paragraph shows how to care for a garden. Soil needs to be cared for in a certain way so it can help the plants grow.

4. **B** The text says, "In response to the First Lady's passion for healthy eating, people across the country have started vegetable gardens at home." When the First Lady planted a vegetable garden, other people decided to plant gardens, too.

5. **Part A**   **A**

    Part B   **H**   A "master" is someone who is an expert on a specific topic. So a "master gardener" is someone who is an expert on gardening. The text says "even if you don't," which means that you do not need to be an expert to grow a garden.

Answer Key

6. Sample answer: The text says that "growing gardens is a great way to learn where food comes from." The text also says it's a way to spend time with others and to eat healthier food.

Unit 11

pages 54–57

1. Sample answer: The word "national" means something having to do with a whole nation or country. Paragraph 2 talks about all "American workers," so the paragraph is describing a holiday that would be celebrated across the whole nation by all Americans.

2. C Peter J. McGuire came up with the idea and shared it with the Central Labor Union. He was making a suggestion.

**3. Part A   C   **"Marched" means a group of people walked together, usually with a purpose or shared reason.

   **Part B   H   **The phrase "ten thousand workers" shows that many people were marching together. This detail supports answer choice C in Part A.

4. A In paragraph 1, the phrase "other workers" suggests that a "union" is a group of workers.

5. B, C The word "legislation" means a "rule" or a "law." The paragraph states that the legislation was passed by Congress.

6. Sample answer: Labor Day is important because it honors workers for their achievements. It is also a day to discuss concerns about working conditions and salaries.

Unit 12

pages 58–61

1. Sample answer: "Sensations" are the feelings created by the body. The text says "no one wants to feel these sensations" and that "pain is a very important reaction of your body."

**2. A, C   **The author used the word "shouts" to show that pain is difficult to ignore. It sends a very strong message.

**3. A, B   **"Messengers" pick up messages from the body and carry these messages into the spinal cord and up into the brain.

4. Sample answer: Nobody wants to have pain. However, it can warn us to protect our bodies.

5. A People with a high tolerance for pain can handle more of it without stopping. This is good for someone who likes to do extreme sports, which can be very painful and tough on the body.

**6. Part A   B   **In this text, a "scale" is a "measure."

   **Part B   E   **A pain scale measures the level of a patient's pain. The pain scale runs from 1 to 10.

Answer Key

Unit 13

pages 62–65

1. Sample answer: "Inactivity" means the "state of not moving." Animals in a state of inactivity breathe slowly and sleep for a long time.

2. **B** The main idea of the text is hibernation. So "hibernation" is the word you should enter into a search engine. The other words cover too much information.

3. **D** The author says that food is most scarce in the winter. Animals eat plants, and plants die in the winter. Animals sleep because food is scarce, or not there. From the context of the paragraph, I know that "scarce" means "in short supply."

4. **A, C** The first section, "Winter," talks about bats and turtles. The last section, "Who Hibernates?" talks about frogs, prairie dogs, and other animals.

5. **Part A** **B**

   Part B **H** The footnotes define the term "rodents." The only other part of the passage that refers to rodents is the final section, which is not an answer choice in Part A.

6. Sample answer: Do Bears Really Hibernate? The Truth About Bears and Hibernation. The Myth About Bears and Hibernation. Bears Go Into Torpor, Too. A good heading should tell the reader what the section of the text is about.

Unit 14

pages 66–69

1. Sample answer: The author states that Gutenberg created the printing press. The author claims that the printing press is responsible for all the books in the world, and those books gave people access to information.

2. **D** The author uses the word "mastermind" to describe Gutenberg. This word reveals the author's point of view, which is that Gutenberg was a genius and an amazing inventor.

3. **A, D** The author explains that books used to be available or used only by scholars, monks, and the rich. These ideas support the claim that there were fewer books before the printing press.

4. **D** "Movable" means that something is able to be moved. The author explains that movable type allowed printers to "move metal letters around the page."

5. **Part A** **C**

   Part B **E** Gutenberg's printing press enabled the printing profession to grow. Books and newspapers were able to be printed more easily. As a result, more people had access to books and knowledge spread around the world.

6. Sample answer: The printing press makes many types of books available to people. This makes learning easier. As a result, people have the information they need to create other inventions.

Answer Key

Unit 15

pages 70–73

1. Sample answer: Viti Levu is part of the Fiji Islands. It is part of the continent of Oceania in the South Pacific Ocean. It is to the southwest of Vanua Levu.

2. **B** According to the map, the Great Sea Reef is off the northern shores of Vanua Levu.

3. **Part A**   **C**   The passage states that Fiji contains "more than 332 islands."

   Part B   **F**   The map labels Viti Levu and Vanua Levu, but it also shows many tiny islands that are all a part of Fiji.

4. **B** Using the compass on the map, you can determine that a person would need to travel southwest from Vanua Levu to get to Viti Levu.

5. **B, F**   To "ban" means to "make something illegal" or "officially not allow something." In Vanua Levu, the government stopped fishing by making it illegal in certain areas.

6. Sample answer: Both the map and passage state that Rotuma is very far from other islands. Therefore, tourists would have to make a special trip just to get there. The people of Rotuma discourage tourists from visiting the island so as not to bring outside influences. As a result, it might be easy for Rotuma to preserve its culture and keep away outsiders.

Unit 16

pages 74–77

1. Sample answer: The text is about the first time humans walked on the moon. The photograph shows the flag the astronauts placed on the moon. The illustration shows either Armstrong or Aldrin standing in a very desolate and bleak landscape.

2. **B** Paragraphs 1 and 4 state that Neil Armstrong took this photo of Edwin "Buzz" Aldrin.

3. **B** The text does not state any details about the flag, but the photograph shows Aldrin next to an American flag on the moon. This supports answer choice B.

4. **A, D**   The photo shows darkness surrounding the moon, which supports the text detail about the "black sky." Also, the photo shows only sky and rocks around Aldrin. This supports the detail about "no sign of life" on the moon.

5. **Part A**   **B**   A "landscape" is "the way a place or area looks."

   Part B   **G**   The passage and the photo describe a place that looks like a wide, rocky plain. These details reveal the meaning of the word "landscape."

Answer Key

6. Sample answer: The photograph and illustration are similar in that they both show an American astronaut on the moon during the first lunar landing. They are different in that the illustration shows an astronaut standing on the moon alone, and the photograph shows the astronaut next to an American flag, suggesting that the astronaut put this flag on the moon.

Unit 17

pages 78–81

1. Sample answer: Illustrations A and B show that the filling goes on the bottom half of the tortilla. Step 2 says to "spoon filling on the bottom half of the tortilla." The toppings go next to the filling.

2. **A, E** Step 2 says that leaving space around the filling prevents the burrito from getting overfilled. If it's too full, the tortilla may rip.

3. **C** Paragraph 9 (Step 6) says to roll the burrito "snugly," but not "too tight." This context clue reveals that "snugly" means "in a tight way."

4. **D** Illustration D has arrows that show how the tortilla should be rolled from the bottom to the top.

5. **Part A** **C** Step 4 states that sides 1 and 2 should be folded toward the imaginary vertical line.

   Part B **H** Illustration C for Step 4 shows that sides 1 and 2 get folded to the center of the tortilla.

6. Sample answer: Steps 5 and 6 describe rolling the burrito snugly from the bottom. The text says to "roll it again" and "roll it for the last time." The illustration shows the burrito getting rolled together.

Unit 18

pages 82–85

1. Sample answer: The text says that "most butterflies are very bright and colorful," but "moths are usually drab."

2. **C** The cecropia moth has splashes of red on its wings. This makes it brighter in color than other moths.

3. **A, D** Most moths are nocturnal, which means they are awake during the night and asleep during the day.

4. **B** Moths either hold their wings spread out flat or folded over their abdomens. Butterflies, on the other hand, fold their wings straight up their backs.

5. **Part A** **A**

   Part B **H** Butterfly antennae have a long shaft with a bulb on its end—like a club. Moths do not have this characteristic.

6. Sample answer: Members of both species start as caterpillars and then spin protective cases as they go into the pupa stage. A moth spins a cocoon, which is a silk case. A butterfly spins a smooth, hard chrysalis.

Conquer New Standards: Informational Text • Grade 3 • © Newmark Learning, LLC

Answer Key

Unit 19

pages 86–89

1. Sample answer: Flamingos eat brine shrimp. The pink coloring of the brine shrimp turns the flamingos' feathers pink.

2. **A** Brine shrimp eat microscopic algae that contain carotenoids.

3. **C** A cardinal's red color would fade without carotenoids, or plant pigments, it gets from berries.

4. **C, D** Paragraph 5 states that eating large amounts of "carrots and pumpkin" can add an "orange-y" tint to a person's skin.

5. **Part A** **A** "Tint" is another word for "color."

   Part B **E** The word "hue" is another word for a "color" or a "tint."

6. Sample answer: If a canary eats a lot of red pepper, then its yellow feathers might change color. The feathers might turn "deep orange."

Unit 20

pages 90–93

1. Sample answer: The person gives the elder a gift of herbs. He or she passes the herbs with the left hand to the elder's left hand.

2. **D** The passage states that "after the elder gives his permission, preparations begin for a special ceremony."

3. **A, D** Paragraph 4 states that, after a person stands in the prayer circle, a fire will be lit and the elder will pick four guides.

4. (1) **C** A person asks an elder for a new name. (2) **D** The person stands in the middle of a prayer circle. (3) **A** A fire is lit. (4) **B** The elder chooses four witnesses. (5) **E** The elder decides when the new name can be used.

5. **Part A** **C** "Immediately" is a word that indicates time. It means that something will happen without delay.

   Part B **H** We know that the person doesn't get the new name immediately because, "*instead*, the elder will decide when the person is ready to be called by the new name." "Instead" shows that something else happens. That something else is a delay. "Immediately" must mean the opposite of "delay."

6. Sample answer: First, the person must ask an elder for permission to get a new name. Part of that ritual is to give the elder a gift of herbs. Second, a special ceremony occurs. That is when the name is announced. Finally, the recipient of the new name hosts a party to thank everyone who attended.

Answer Key

Unit 21

pages 94–99

1. Sample answer: The first passage refers to Misty Copeland as "Misty." That makes the article seem more friendly, as if the person who wrote it knows her personally. The second passage refers to her as "Copeland." That makes the passage sound more professional and as if the author is an expert who probably does not know her personally.

2. **A** "Misty Copeland Changes the Face of Ballet" talks about the beginning of Copeland's ballet career, when she was 13. We learn about her family life and her rapid advancement as a ballerina.

3. **Part A**   **C**

   Part B   **G**   The text says that the family "struggled." The text describes how she and her family lived in a motel, slept on the floor, and didn't have a car to get places. These details show that they were having a difficult time. These details support the idea that "struggled" must mean "had a difficult time."

4. Sample answer: "Misty Copeland Dances Into History" best shows Copeland's dedication to ballet. It talks about how much she wanted to dance the role of the firebird. She wanted it so badly that she didn't tell anyone she was hurt. The author says, "It was an injury that would have ended the career of many dancers," but Misty's career didn't end. That is dedication.

5. **C** The author could have said that Copeland performed in *The Firebird*. Instead, the author says Copeland gave "a stunning performance." "Stunning" is a positive word. It shows that the author thinks highly of Copeland.

6. (1) **C** Copeland and her family live in a motel. (2) **B** Copeland dances the role of the firebird. (3) **E** Copeland undergoes surgery for a nearly-broken leg. (4) **A** Copeland stars in a commercial. (5) **D** Copeland is named a principal dancer at ABT.

7. **Part A**   **D**

   Part B   **H**   After achieving "many accomplishments in the world of ballet," Misty "faced prejudice from people who thought that only white dancers belonged in ballet." Prejudice is a form of racism, or thinking that one ethnic background is better than another.

8. Sample answer: The last paragraph of "Misty Copeland Changes the Face of Ballet" talks about the prejudice Copeland faced even after she achieved success. There were "people who thought that only white dancers belonged in ballet." That's why it's a big deal that she is the first African American principal dancer at ABT. She is trying to change people's understanding of ballet and how they think ballerinas should look.

     Conquer New Standards: Informational Text · Grade 3 · © Newmark Learning, LLC

Notes

Notes

_____

_____

_____

_____

_____

_____

_____

_____

_____

_____

_____

Conquer New Standards: Informational Text • Grade 3 • © Newmark Learning, LLC

Notes

Notes

Notes

Notes

_____

_____

_____

_____

_____

_____

_____

_____

_____

_____

_____